LEO

2024

Zodiac world, Volume 4

Daniel Sanjurjo

Published by Daniel Sanjurjo, 2023.

While every precaution has been taken in the preparation of this book, the publisher assumes no responsibility for errors or omissions, or for damages resulting from the use of the information contained herein.

ISBN: 9798866921577

First edition. November 8, 2023.

Written by Daniel Sanjurjo.

LEO

Radiant Leo: A Comprehensive Zodiac Guide

Introduction:

Welcome to a captivating journey into the heart of Leo, the regal ruler of the zodiac. In these pages, we unveil the mysteries, passions, and unique qualities that define the charismatic individuals born under the sign of the Lion. Whether you're a Leo seeking deeper self-understanding or an inquisitive soul eager to explore the Leo in your life, this book is your comprehensive guide to the world of this fiery and magnetic sign.

Our exploration begins with the highly anticipated horoscope for the year 2024, offering Leo readers valuable insights into what the cosmos has in store. From love to career, health to personal growth, this horoscope will help you navigate the challenges and opportunities that lie ahead.

But this book is more than just an annual forecast. It's a holistic view of Leo's personality and how this sun sign shapes their identity. We delve into the core characteristics that make Leos stand out in the zodiac, from their unwavering confidence to their warm-hearted generosity.

You'll discover the influence of Leo's ruling celestial body and how it colors their approach to life. Through in-depth analysis, we explore how Leos navigate relationships, both romantic and

platonic, as well as their career paths, where their natural leadership abilities often shine.

As we journey through these pages, you'll gain a profound understanding of Leo's emotional landscape, creative tendencies, and the unique challenges they may encounter. With each chapter, you'll find yourself drawn closer to the captivating world of the Leo zodiac sign.

So, whether you're a Leo seeking to embrace your full potential or someone who wants to unravel the enigma of the Lion, this book promises to be your trusted companion on this remarkable voyage. Let's embark on this exploration of Leo, where the stars align with your destiny, and the heart of the Lion beats with boundless passion.

An In-Depth Insight

The year 2024 brings a plethora of possibilities and challenges for those born under the Leo sign. This horoscope is tailored specifically for Leo individuals, aiming to provide a comprehensive understanding of the celestial influences that will shape your life in the coming year.

The financial aspect is a crucial focus for the Leo Horoscope 2024. It raises questions about your financial stability for the year. Will your finances remain steady, or will you encounter challenges? The prospects of acquiring property and vehicles are also under scrutiny. Understanding the financial landscape will be vital as it directly impacts various facets of your life.

The horoscope doesn't just stop at finances; it also offers insights into your romantic relationships. It delves into the timing of ups and downs in your love life. Moments of joy and potential challenges are highlighted, guiding you in navigating the intricacies of your romantic connections.

Family plays a pivotal role in our lives, and this horoscope explores whether your family life will be filled with happiness or beset by problems. It touches upon the dynamics of your relationships with family members and sheds light on what to expect in your familial sphere.

Your career is another essential aspect under the astrological lens. The direction your career will take in 2024 is a matter of significant interest. Will you experience progress and success, or are setbacks on the horizon? This horoscope seeks to provide insights into the potential course of your professional life.

Furthermore, it offers an opportunity to assess the status of your relationships with loved ones. For married individuals, it can help determine whether harmony will prevail in your married life. Your health status for the year is also addressed, emphasizing the need for self-care and well-being.

This horoscope has been carefully prepared by astrologer Dr. Mrigank, an expert in astrology, based on Vedic astrology principles. It takes into account the impact of planetary transits and movements on the lives of Leo individuals. It's essential to note that this horoscope is specifically crafted for those born under the Leo sign based on their moon sign.

Saturn, present in the seventh house from the beginning, is predicted to create opportunities for business growth. It will also bring harmony to your married life and empower your life partner to become a clear communicator. The emphasis in 2024 lies on moving forward with discipline, and it is during this time that Saturn is expected to bless you with benefits.

Additionally, you'll have ample chances to embark on long journeys and explore opportunities for foreign travel. Jupiter, residing in the ninth house from the beginning of the year until the first of May, is expected to equip you with the ability to make sound decisions. It will bring news related to the happiness of your children, and your mind will be occupied with engaging in good deeds, along with a keen interest in charity, religion, and accumulating merits.

While the year holds promise, there's also a need to pay attention to your health. Rahu's presence in your eighth house throughout the year suggests the importance of being cautious. Furthermore, exercising caution while driving is essential. According to the Leo yearly horoscope 2024, your father may experience health issues from time to time, so it is important to take care of his well-being. On a positive note, there will be favorable planetary combinations within your family, promoting peace and goodwill. Therefore, during the first half of the year, it's advisable to focus on maintaining strong relationships with yourself, your life partner, and your business partners. By adhering to discipline and being mindful of your health, you can ensure a healthy year ahead.

For Love

In matters of the heart, the Leo Horoscope 2024 paints a vivid picture of the romantic journey that Leo individuals are likely to embark on in the coming year.

At the outset of the year, it's predicted that Leo individuals may encounter initial challenges in their romantic relationships. The fifth house, where matters of love and romance reside, will be influenced by the energetic presence of the Sun and Mars. This alignment can potentially bring about moments of passion and intensity, but it may also introduce its own set of challenges. However, the divine teacher, Jupiter, will cast its benevolent gaze over the fifth house from the ninth house, offering a glimmer of hope even in the face of these potential difficulties.

The Leo Horoscope 2024 advises maintaining a calm and peaceful demeanor during this time, dedicating ample time to each other to resolve misunderstandings and strengthen the bond between partners through open and honest discussions. The early months of the year, specifically February and March, hold the promise of favorable circumstances for love and romance, bringing moments of joy and connection.

As the year unfolds, the influence of Venus and Mercury in your love life becomes increasingly apparent. These planetary alignments are predicted to enhance the depth of your romantic connections, fostering a sense of deeper affection and understanding between you and your partner. This period signifies the maturation of your relationship, characterized by a deeper and more profound bond.

However, caution is advised during August and September. These months may introduce potential challenges in your love life. Issues with your beloved might arise, and external pressures, possibly from family members, could affect your relationship. During this time, it's essential to remain vigilant and express your true feelings to your partner. Maintaining open lines of communication while exercising caution is crucial to weathering these potential storms and providing unwavering support to your loved one.

The latter part of the year, particularly after September, is expected to be more favorable for your romantic life. During this time, you and your beloved are likely to experience the complete bliss of your love relationship. As your connection deepens, you'll find yourselves striving to give your relationship a meaningful name, symbolizing the progress you've made in your journey together.

The Leo Horoscope 2024 provides a roadmap for the ups and downs in your romantic life throughout the year, guiding you in navigating the complexities of love, building stronger bonds, and finding moments of pure joy with your beloved.

For Career

The Leo Horoscope 2024 presents an intriguing forecast for the career prospects of individuals born under this zodiac sign. The year is expected to kick off on a positive note, with several planetary influences contributing to your professional growth and success.

Saturn, a powerful presence, is forecasted to be strong in the tenth house from the beginning of the year and will continue to exert its influence throughout the year. This positioning of Saturn, which is the ruler of the seventh house, signifies a period of potential success in your career. Your hard work and dedication are predicted to yield favorable results, ultimately strengthening your position in your current job or profession.

The Leo Career Horoscope 2024 highlights the early months of the year, with the influence of Mercury and Venus on your tenth house. This alignment suggests that you will have a clear opportunity to excel in your profession. It signifies a time when you can showcase your skills and make significant advancements in your career. These planetary influences act as stepping stones for professional growth, and your efforts are likely to be rewarded with success.

Jupiter, the planet associated with expansion and opportunities, is poised to reside in your ninth house until May 1st. This positioning opens the door to potential job changes and transfers during the first two months of the year. If you are employed in a government service, there may be opportunities for relocation or transfers to new locations. This period also holds promise for individuals who have been contemplating a change in their current job. Your desire for a job change may find fulfillment during the initial quarter of the year, making a job transition a real possibility.

The Leo Career Horoscope 2024 further anticipates the presence of Mars, the planet of energy and action, in your ninth house from June 1st to July 12th. Subsequently, Mars will move to your tenth house until August 26th. This positioning of Mars holds the potential to bring forth favorable job opportunities, particularly following a job transition. The month of July is expected to be characterized by a bustling and active work environment. During this period, you may have the opportunity to undertake work-related travels or even consider relocating to a different city or state for professional reasons.

While the period between July 31st and August 25th may present some challenges, it is crucial to remain diligent and work hard during this phase to overcome any obstacles. The latter part of the year, specifically from October to November, promises excellent conditions in your job. Additionally, there is a possibility of another job change in the final month of the year, which could lead to exciting career developments.

In conclusion, the Leo Horoscope 2024 paints a promising picture for your career. With Saturn's strong influence, the support of Jupiter, and the energy of Mars, you have the potential to attain a favorable position in your current job and achieve success in transitioning to new employment opportunities throughout the year. This year offers the chance for professional growth, advancement, and exciting career changes, so be prepared to make the most of these opportunities.

For Education

The Leo Horoscope 2024 for education offers insights and guidance for students born under the Leo zodiac sign as they embark on their academic journey in the upcoming year.

The year 2024 may begin with some initial challenges for Leo students, but the planetary movements suggest that your dedication and commitment to your studies will be unwavering. Mercury and Venus are positioned in the fourth house, while Jupiter graces the ninth house, instilling a natural interest in education and setting the stage for positive academic results right from the start of the year.

Your enthusiasm for learning will be evident, and your efforts will be directed toward achieving your educational goals. However, it's worth noting that the presence of the Sun and Mars in the fifth house, along with Saturn's influence on the fourth house, may introduce occasional obstacles and disruptions that could affect your concentration and create some difficulties in your educational pursuits.

The Leo Horoscope 2024 anticipates that starting in April, the planetary transits will align more favorably, ushering in circumstances that are conducive to effective and focused studying. As the year progresses, you can expect improved conditions for your educational endeavors.

For those Leo individuals preparing for competitive exams in 2024, the period from February to March is predicted to be highly favorable. If you have diligently put in efforts, this period can bring exceptional success and may even lead to selection for a specific government service. Additionally, the period between August and November is also expected to be advantageous, with strong planetary alignments that can yield positive results in competitive exams.

If you have aspirations for higher education, the first half of the year, as indicated by the Leo Horoscope 2024, offers more favorable conditions. This period provides you with an opportunity to pursue the higher education you desire. While studying abroad might encounter some delays, your desire to do so can still be fulfilled. After August, there may be opportunities to pursue your higher education goals abroad, presenting exciting prospects for your academic journey.

In summary, the Leo Horoscope 2024 for education acknowledges the initial challenges that may arise but assures you that your dedication and determination will lead to academic success. The year holds promise for competitive exam success and opportunities for higher education, both domestically and potentially abroad. Your commitment to your studies and your ability to adapt to changing circumstances will be your keys to a successful academic year.

For Finances

THE LEO HOROSCOPE FOR 2024 provides valuable insights into your financial prospects for the year, shedding light on what you can expect in terms of income and expenses.

In the realm of finances, it's crucial for Leo individuals to approach the year with caution. The planetary alignment indicates that while there are possibilities for income generation, you'll also need to contend with ongoing expenses. This balance between income and expenditure is vital to maintaining financial stability.

The presence of Ketu in your second house and Rahu in the eighth house throughout the year introduces complexity into your financial situation. These planetary positions can lead to various types of expenditures, making it challenging to maintain a stable financial footing. It's essential to be mindful of your financial decisions and expenses, as mismanagement can lead to financial imbalances.

However, there is a silver lining. The period from April to August holds the potential for favorable financial outcomes. During this time, you may have strong opportunities for financial gains, which can help offset the challenges posed by the planetary positions earlier in the year. It's a time when you can make wise financial decisions and work towards strengthening your financial position.

For the remaining months of the year, it becomes even more critical to utilize your resources wisely. The key to financial stability is prudent financial management. Failing to do so may result in difficulties and imbalances throughout the year. By making conscious efforts to control your expenses, save, and invest wisely, you can navigate the financial challenges and work towards achieving financial equilibrium.

In summary, the Leo Horoscope 2024 for finances emphasizes the importance of caution and financial prudence. While there may be periods of financial opportunity, the year, overall, requires careful financial planning and management to ensure that you maintain a stable and balanced financial situation. By exercising wisdom in your financial decisions, you can navigate the complexities and work towards financial stability.

For Family life

In the realm of family life, the Leo Horoscope for 2024 brings a mix of experiences throughout the year.

At the beginning of the year, the presence of Ketu in your second house may introduce some challenges within your family. This could disrupt the harmony in your relationships and lead to familial issues that require attention. However, the planetary positions also offer positive influences, with Venus and Mercury in your fourth house. These influences amplify the joys and comforts of your family life. Your family members will be a source of support, and your home will be a place of peace and happiness. During this time, you can expect improvements in your living conditions and an overall sense of contentment. The atmosphere at home will be delightful and conducive to positive family interactions.

As the year progresses, a significant event occurs on May 1st when Jupiter, often referred to as the divine teacher, enters your tenth house. This positioning of Jupiter will offer valuable insights regarding your second and fourth houses, directly impacting your family life. This celestial movement is set to enhance the happiness and tranquility within your family, bringing positive changes.

The Leo Horoscope 2024 also suggests that during the first half of the year, you will establish harmonious and positive relationships with your siblings. This period is marked by positive interactions with brothers and sisters, fostering strong bonds.

In the second half of the year, the focus shifts to your parents. You can anticipate favorable relations with your parents during this time, strengthening the familial bonds and creating a supportive environment within your family.

It's important to be attentive to your father's health from March to June, as there is a possibility of him experiencing health issues during this period. Your care and support during this time can contribute to his well-being and the overall harmony of your family.

In summary, the Leo Horoscope 2024 for family life suggests a year of mixed experiences, with some challenges at the beginning, but with the potential for positive changes and harmonious family relationships as the year progresses. Your family will play a significant role in providing support and happiness throughout the year, and your attention to their well-being, especially your father's health, is advised.

For Children

When it comes to your children, the Leo Horoscope for 2024 offers insights into their prospects and behaviors throughout the year.

In the first half of the year, there's a favorable alignment for those who desire to have offspring. Jupiter, often referred to as the divine teacher, will reside in your ninth house until May 1st. During this period, Jupiter's influence is directed toward your first and fifth houses. This alignment of planetary energy carries strong indications of the birth of a well-behaved and virtuous child, bringing immense joy and happiness to your life. If you've been hoping to expand your family, this could be a particularly favorable time.

However, for those who already have children, the beginning of the year may present some challenges. The presence of the Sun and Mars in the fifth house can amplify the inherent traits of your children. As a result, they may exhibit a bit of stubbornness, making it challenging to maintain discipline and have them heed your words. They might assert their own will more strongly during this time. Nevertheless, the period between February and March will bring a positive shift. Your children will develop a sense of love, respect, and empathy towards you during these months.

As the year progresses, specifically from April to August, you can expect a relatively stable phase concerning your children. During this time, you'll receive occasional positive indications regarding your children's progress and well-being. They will adapt well to their chosen paths, make significant strides, and you might receive news of a suitable marriage proposal for one of them, which will bring added happiness and contentment to your household.

In summary, the Leo Horoscope 2024 for children predicts a year marked by the potential for the birth of well-behaved and virtuous offspring, particularly in the first half of the year. If you already have children, they may display some stubbornness initially, but they will grow to demonstrate love and respect. As the year unfolds, your children are likely to make positive progress in various aspects of their lives, contributing to the overall happiness of your family.

For Married Life

The Leo Horoscope for 2024 provides valuable insights into your married life and the dynamics you can expect throughout the year.

Married individuals will find that Saturn remains in their seventh house for the entire year. This placement signifies that life partners will hold strong opinions and exert determined efforts to achieve their goals and decisions. However, it's worth noting that the presence of Rahu in the eighth house introduces an interesting dynamic. It suggests some level of support from the in-laws, although there may be instances when they don't fully follow through on their promises, which can be a bit disheartening at times.

The Leo Horoscope for 2024 also highlights a specific period of caution, spanning from February to June. During this time, Mars will be transiting through both the seventh and eighth houses, where Saturn and Rahu are already positioned. This celestial configuration could potentially lead to health issues for life partners. Additionally, there might be an increase in tension between spouses, and relationships with in-laws could become strained.

However, there's positive news as the year unfolds. According to the horoscope, love and affection will begin to blossom in your married life starting in July. You and your partner will gradually rekindle your affection for each other during this period. The real highlight comes between August and November, during which your married life is expected to be filled with happiness and harmonious moments.

For those who are unmarried, the first and second quarters of the year will see discussions and deliberations about marriage taking place within your family. There's a significant chance that your proposal may find acceptance, indicating the potential for a new chapter in your life.

In summary, the Leo Horoscope 2024 suggests that married individuals will experience a mix of strong opinions and determined efforts from their life partners, with some support from in-laws, though not always consistent. The year might have a challenging period from February to June but will then see a resurgence of love and happiness in married life from July onwards. For the unmarried Leo individuals, there is a good chance of marriage discussions and potential acceptance of marriage proposals in the early part of the year.

For Business

The Leo Business Horoscope for 2024 brings promising prospects for your business ventures.

Saturn, the ruler of the seventh house, will remain in the seventh house throughout the year, setting the stage for favorable conditions for long-term profitability. This celestial alignment indicates that your business will gradually expand, and the rewards it offers will come steadily and effortlessly, ensuring substantial outcomes. As the year progresses, you can expect your business to advance and grow.

However, it's essential to exercise caution due to the presence of Rahu in the eighth house. The first half of the year might present comparatively weaker circumstances as Mars and the Sun transit through your sixth and seventh houses. During this period, you may encounter challenges in your professional partnerships. But if you can successfully navigate these obstacles, your business is poised to thrive as the year unfolds.

The real highlights for your business come between July and October. During this time frame, you can anticipate notable advancements in your business, along with significant changes that will contribute to its growth and success.

In summary, the Leo Business Horoscope for 2024 predicts a year of gradual but steady business expansion, with the potential for long-term profits. While challenges may arise, especially in the first half of the year, your ability to overcome them will lead to thriving business prospects.

The period from July to October is particularly auspicious for notable advancements and growth in your business.

For Property and Vehicle

The Leo Horoscope for 2024 indicates a promising outlook for your financial situation, particularly concerning property and vehicles.

At the beginning of the year, your fourth house will be influenced by both Venus and Mercury, creating a favorable environment for you to consider acquiring a new vehicle. This new vehicle will not only offer comfort and amenities but will also align with your specific preferences for features and durability. The prime opportunities for purchasing a new vehicle will be during the periods of January to February and again from August to November.

Furthermore, the middle part of the year, from June to August, holds the potential for substantial wealth accumulation, particularly in the form of immovable assets. This period will present favorable conditions for lucrative financial transactions that will significantly enhance your financial standing. You will have the ability to utilize your skills to invest additional funds and acquire valuable assets during this timeframe.

In summary, the Leo Horoscope for 2024 suggests that you can expect a prosperous year in terms of property and vehicles. The specified time frames offer excellent opportunities for acquiring a new vehicle, and the middle part of the year is conducive to accumulating substantial wealth, especially in the form of

immovable assets, which will contribute to your financial wellbeing.

For Wealth

The Leo Horoscope for 2024 brings both challenges and opportunities on the financial front.

Throughout the year, Rahu, the celestial entity, will be present in your eighth house, which may lead to increased expenses and financial turbulence. This suggests that you will need to spend money on various aspects of your life. On the other hand, until May 1st, Jupiter, the divine planet, will reside in your ninth house, guiding you in making sound decisions.

However, it's important to note that Jupiter's influence will also be influenced by Saturn. This influence may lead to pilgrimages and long journeys in the first half of the year, which can have both positive and negative financial implications. While these travels can potentially benefit your business and lead to lucrative contracts, they may also bring significant expenses. Caution and financial planning will be crucial during this period.

The first half of the year may require heightened vigilance, especially when it comes to making investments between March and June, as hasty decisions could lead to financial losses and distress. However, if you proceed with caution, the latter half of the year appears more favorable. During this time, there will be opportunities to accumulate wealth and improve your financial situation. Those who are employed may witness positive changes in their careers, potentially resulting in better salaries and financial gains.

In summary, the Leo Horoscope for 2024 suggests a year with financial challenges and opportunities. The presence of Rahim in your eighth house may lead to increased expenses, but the guidance of Jupiter and the potential for business-related gains during the first half of the year should not be overlooked. It's essential to exercise caution in your financial decisions, particularly during the first half of the year, and be prepared for positive changes and financial improvements in the latter part of the year.

For Health

The Leo Horoscope for 2024 indicates that your health may face some challenges during the initial phase of the year, and it's crucial to exercise caution in health-related matters. Several planetary influences can impact your well-being, including the Sun in the fifth house, Saturn in the seventh house, and Rahu in the eighth house.

The presence of the Sun in the fifth house suggests that you should pay attention to potential health issues that could affect your vitality and overall well-being. Additionally, Saturn in the seventh house and Rahu in the eighth house may contribute to occasional health concerns. These planetary positions may lead to the sudden emergence of temporary health problems, causing discomfort for a limited duration.

The first half of the year is expected to be relatively weaker in terms of health, and you may encounter issues related to your blood, stomach, fever, and headaches during this period. To mitigate these health challenges, it's advised to make substantial changes in your daily routine. Leading a disciplined life, including maintaining a balanced diet and nutrition, will be essential in avoiding many health problems.

In summary, the Leo Horoscope for 2024 suggests that while the year may bring some health challenges, especially during the first half, you can take proactive steps to maintain your well-being. Paying attention to your diet, nutrition, and adopting a disciplined lifestyle can help you avoid potential health issues and promote overall health and vitality.

Lucky Number For Leo In 2024

In 2024, Leo individuals are associated with the lucky numbers 1 and 9. The ruling planet for your zodiac sign is the powerful Sun, which imparts its energy and influence on your life. The total score for the year is 8, suggesting that 2024 will be a year that requires your personal efforts to overcome challenges and achieve your goals.

Leo Horoscope 2024 emphasizes the importance of focusing on your financial and physical well-being. While there may be challenges in various aspects of life, you can anticipate relatively better outcomes in these areas. It's advisable to preserve your self-esteem and avoid unnecessary conflicts with others. By maintaining a positive outlook and putting in the necessary effort, you can make the most of the opportunities that come your way in 2024.

MONTH BY MONTH

January 2024 Horoscope: Leo

The Leo horoscope for January 2024 foresees significant changes in career and business ventures. Initiating a new professional role at the beginning of the year is auspicious, with successful outcomes expected in business development endeavors. For Leos, familial harmony greatly influences self-esteem, but the Sun in Capricorn introduces a period of restraint, possibly leading to a chill in relationships. Active efforts are needed to counter this negative trend. Single Leos can anticipate favorable romantic adventures, especially during the Wolf Full Moon in January, prompting them to take the initiative, including exploring online dating.

Early January demands the ability to adapt to challenging situations, as unexpected expenses may arise, requiring an economic approach. The horoscope advises Leos to rely on their strengths and conduct a financial audit to manage even a modest budget effectively. Venus in Sagittarius fosters positive thinking, ensuring swift resolution of challenges. Despite hurdles, Leo remains determined to lead an interesting life, finding joy in simple pleasures like friendly gatherings, trips, or thematic quests.

By mid-month, the festive spirit diminishes, giving way to despondency, particularly for those with lower adaptive abilities struggling to return to their previous routines. The general Leo horoscope for January 2024 anticipates a dip in well-being, emphasizing the need to care for the cardiovascular system and consume foods rich in potassium and magnesium. Mercury in Capricorn ensures minimal losses, and Leo can effectively address challenges as they arise.

The end of January witnesses a career upswing, with startups rapidly advancing. Leos are advised to adopt a swift and meticulous approach, capitalizing on the support of Mars in Capricorn for discipline and effective weight management.

Additional Monthly Insights for Leo:

- Love Horoscope: The alignment of celestial bodies suggests favorable conditions for romantic pursuits, especially during the Wolf Full Moon. Leos are encouraged to take the initiative, and online dating may prove fruitful.
- Professional Horoscope: The beginning of the year marks a favorable time for new career endeavors and business development. Leos should seize opportunities and take calculated risks.
- Finances: Unexpected expenses may require a shift to an economy mode. Conducting a financial audit and planning diligently will help Leos stay within their budget.
- Family: The restrained influence of the Sun in Capricorn may impact familial relationships. Active efforts are needed to maintain warmth and harmony within the family.
- Children: Leos with children should pay attention to their well-being and emotional needs during the month. Quality time spent together can strengthen the parent-child bond.

- Business: Entrepreneurs and business owners may experience positive developments in their ventures. Swift and decisive actions are recommended for success.
- Money and Gains: Despite challenges, positive thinking will lead to swift resolution and minimal financial losses. Leo's ability to adapt will contribute to financial stability.
- Health: Mid-month may bring a dip in well-being. Leo should prioritize cardiovascular health and include foods rich in potassium and magnesium in their diet.
- Astrological Aspects: The alignment of Pluto in Aquarius highlights financial matters, emphasizing the need for organization and productivity. The eclipse in March signifies a period of culmination and liberation.

February 2024 Horoscope: Leo

The Leo horoscope for February 2024 brings a surge of positive energy and exciting opportunities. It's a month when luck aligns with your endeavors, urging you to broaden your horizons and explore new creative projects. The influence of the Sun in Aquarius propels your desire for progress, requiring a systematic approach to organize your ideas. It's a time to shed outdated thoughts that hinder your progress and to eliminate negative influences from your surroundings.

Family and Lunar Influences

Early February places a spotlight on family connections. Your close ones become a wellspring of inspiration, providing warmth and home comfort. According to the Leo horoscope, spending quality time with your family will be a priceless gift. While your natural instinct might be to tackle difficult situations head-on, Venus in Capricorn advises a measured approach, allowing negotiations and meetings to unfold smoothly.

Productivity Surge and Self-Reflection

Mid-February marks a highly productive period, fueled by an overflow of energy. You'll tackle challenges that once seemed insurmountable. The general Leo horoscope for February 2024 predicts a peak in self-esteem due to your achievements. Don't hesitate to invest in status items to maintain your image. Mercury in Aquarius subtly encourages a reevaluation of values, opening doors to newfound interests and changes in habits.

Perseverance and Career Advancements

As February draws to a close, your perseverance yields substantial rewards. The horoscope suggests that continuous learning is key to a successful career. Leverage the chance to secure an internship in a reputable company. Despite the subconscious influence of Mars in Aquarius, creating a sense of unpredictability, your determined approach can overcome challenges. Be mindful of maintaining inner balance to avoid physical ailments.

Additional Monthly Insights for Leo:

- Love Horoscope: The alignment of celestial bodies suggests favorable conditions for romantic pursuits, especially during the Wolf Full Moon. Leos are encouraged to take the initiative, and online dating may prove fruitful.
- Professional Horoscope: The beginning of the year marks a favorable time for new career endeavors and business development. Leos should seize opportunities and take calculated risks.
- Finances: Unexpected expenses may require a shift to an economy mode. Conducting a financial audit and planning diligently will help Leos stay within their budget.
- Family: The restrained influence of the Sun in Capricorn may impact familial relationships. Active efforts are needed to maintain warmth and harmony within the family.
- Children: Leos with children should pay attention to their well-being and emotional needs during the

month. Quality time spent together can strengthen the parent-child bond.

- Business: Entrepreneurs and business owners may experience positive developments in their ventures. Swift and decisive actions are recommended for success.

- Money and Gains: Despite challenges, positive thinking will lead to swift resolution and minimal financial losses. Leo's ability to adapt will contribute to financial stability.

- Health: Mid-month may bring a dip in well-being. Leo should prioritize cardiovascular health and include foods rich in potassium and magnesium in their diet.

- Astrological Aspects: The alignment of Pluto in Aquarius highlights financial matters, emphasizing the need for organization and productivity. The eclipse in March signifies a period of culmination and liberation.

March 2024 Horoscope: Leo

The Leo horoscope for March 2024 promises a surge of enthusiasm. Spring warmth awakens dormant forces, giving impetus to development in various life areas, including personal growth. However, the potential obstacle lies in the frequent changes in mood, attributed to the Sun in Pisces casting a pessimistic view, leading to heightened anxiety for Leo. To restore spiritual harmony, meditation is recommended.

Surprises and Dramatic Changes with the Worm Full Moon

The Worm Full Moon in March brings surprises, signifying possible dramatic changes in personal life. Lonely Leos may find true love, and decisions to marry quickly after meeting an ideal partner are likely.

Fast-Paced Initiatives and New Directions

The initial days of March set a fast pace, demanding individuals to match its rhythm. Despite the hustle, life proceeds according to a clear schedule. The Leo horoscope advises trying new directions, such as venturing into science or creativity, without fearing failure. With the influence of Venus in Aquarius, communication becomes a joy, even with challenging individuals. Leo proves to be an interesting interlocutor, capable of engaging in conversations on various topics. Intuition is crucial to navigate situations smoothly.

Financial Caution and Constructive Dialogues

Regarding finances, the middle of the month doesn't bring significant changes, and the situation remains predictable. Money flows in as scheduled, and salary delays are unlikely. The general Leo horoscope for March 2024 recommends adhering to a budget, cautioning against large purchases or investments. Mercury in Aries enhances the gift of persuasion, empowering Leo to be a brilliant speaker. Constructive dialogues can be established, but potential sharp moments act as litmus tests for relationships. Addressing painful topics is crucial for long-term stability.

Fruitful Creativity and Collaboration

The concluding days of March unfold rapidly, proving most fruitful for those in the arts who can find beauty in ordinary things. The Leo horoscope foresees a rich creative process, allowing for the completion of lingering projects and the initiation of new ideas, preferably through collaboration. Despite Leo's proud nature, the influence of Mars in Pisces may introduce doubts. However, this effect also activates imagination, offering opportunities for experimentation, such as trying different shades of hair.

Additional Monthly Insights for Leo:

- Love Horoscope: The alignment of celestial bodies suggests favorable conditions for romantic pursuits, especially during the Worm Full Moon. Leos are encouraged to take the initiative, and online dating may prove fruitful.

- Professional Horoscope: March is marked by a surge of enthusiasm, making it conducive to breakthroughs in various life areas, including personal development. Embrace new directions and creative endeavors.

- Finances: The middle of the month brings no significant financial changes. Stick to your budget, avoiding large purchases or investments. Mercury in Aries enhances persuasion skills for financial negotiations.

- Family: The initial days emphasize family connections, providing inspiration and comfort. Maintain a measured approach, allowing smooth negotiations and meetings.

- Children: Pay attention to children's well-being and emotional needs during the month. Quality time spent together strengthens the parent-child bond.

- Business: The fast-paced initial days set the tone for productive ventures. March favors trying new directions, especially in science or creativity. Communication is key, and intuition aids in navigating challenges.

- Money and Gains: Financial stability is maintained by adhering to the budget. Positive thinking and adaptability contribute to resolving challenges with minimal financial losses.

- Health: Be cautious of a potential dip in well-being mid-month. Prioritize cardiovascular health and include potassium and magnesium-rich foods in your diet.

- Astrological Aspects: The alignment of Pluto in Aquarius emphasizes financial matters, highlighting the importance of organization and productivity. The eclipse in March signifies a period of culmination and liberation.

April 2024 Horoscope: Leo

The Leo horoscope for April 2024 radiates optimism, bringing positive career changes and financial successes. However, amidst these successes, it's crucial for Leo not to become overly dreamy, as inflated self-esteem could lead to disappointments. With the Sun in Aries emphasizing leadership, balancing ambitions with realistic opportunities becomes essential to avoid unnecessary setbacks.

Career and Financial Successes

The beginning of April unfolds in a calm and spiritually comfortable manner for Leo. Harmonious interactions with others, coupled with financial prosperity, create a positive atmosphere. According to the Leo horoscope, financial gains surpass expectations, possibly through a job promotion with a higher salary or recognition from authorities for achievements. With the influence of Venus in Aries, encouraging impulsive actions, Leo's vibrant imagination takes center stage. This period offers an excellent opportunity for experimenting with one's image, and even unconventional outfits will find their place. It's a time to proudly declare exclusivity to the world.

Family Harmony After the Pink Full Moon

Family relationships experience a warming trend after the Pink Full Moon in April, fostering reconciliation. The supportive energy of this moon positively impacts Leo's emotional state, naturally resolving reasons for quarrels. By mid-month, family storms subside, affirming the effectiveness of Leo's chosen behavioral approach.

Gentleness towards loved ones doesn't imply indifference but reflects a desire to cultivate a harmonious life. The general Leo horoscope for April 2024 deems it a convenient moment for educational conversations, especially if children are facing challenging decisions. With Mercury in Aries enhancing the gift of persuasion, Leo's ability to engage in constructive dialogues is heightened, leading to successful outcomes.

Balancing Pride and Self-Care

As the month concludes, a breakdown signals potential exorbitant loads. While financial and career successes evoke pride, it's essential for Leo to recognize the limits of their endurance. The April horoscope suggests a risk of sliding into apathy, emphasizing the importance of taking a break. Despite Leo's proud character, the influence of Mars in Pisces prompts a reevaluation, introducing doubt. This shift also activates the imagination, providing opportunities for positive use. Experimentation, such as trying different shades of hair, becomes a viable outlet.

Additional Monthly Insights for Leo:

- Love Horoscope: The Pink Full Moon fosters a positive shift in family relationships, promoting emotional well-being. Reconciliation is facilitated, and quarrels naturally dissipate.

- Professional Horoscope: April brings positive career changes and financial successes for Leo. Balancing ambitions with realistic opportunities is crucial under the leadership-focused influence of the Sun in Aries.

- Finances: Financial gains exceed expectations in the beginning. The impulsive influence of Venus in Aries allows Leo to express their vibrant imagination and experiment with their image.

- Family: The Pink Full Moon signifies a harmonious period in family relationships, aiding reconciliation. Mid-month provides a convenient time for educational conversations, especially with children facing decisions.

- Children: Educational conversations with children are favored in April. Mercury in Aries enhances persuasion skills, making it easier for Leo to guide and advise effectively.

- Business: Positive career changes and financial successes mark the beginning of April. Leo's vibrant imagination is an asset, allowing experimentation with their image.

- Money and Gains: Financial gains surpass expectations, possibly through a job promotion or recognition from authorities. It's a time of financial prosperity for Leo.

- Health: Recognize potential overexertion in the last days of April. Taking a break is essential to avoid sliding into apathy. Acknowledge personal limits and prioritize self-care.

- Astrological Aspects: The influence of Mars in Pisces prompts a reevaluation of Leo's limits and endurance. The activated imagination provides opportunities for positive use, such as experimenting with appearance.

May 2024 Horoscope: Leo

The Leo horoscope for May 2024 promises a season of love victories, with compliments and invitations for dates coming from all directions. The powerful influence of the Sun in Taurus provides perseverance and a surge of energy, fueling Leo's desire to realize ambitions. However, attention from the opposite sex may pose challenges for those in relationships, requiring careful navigation to avoid complications. The Flower Full Moon in May heightens emotions, cautioning against touchiness that could hinder connections with influential individuals. Leo must embrace humility to foster successful interactions.

Mood Swings and Perseverance

The initial days of May bring unpredictable mood swings. Leo may experience moments of beauty followed by unbearable challenges. The horoscope advises acceptance of the fact that success might not be immediate, suggesting a temporary pause to gain clarity. Under the influence of Venus in Taurus, stability graces the world, making goals more tangible. Leo may adopt a slightly conservative stance, showcasing a caring nature through gifts and kind words. This shift in reputation contributes to an elevated standing in the eyes of others.

New Opportunities and Housing Solutions

The middle of May unveils new opportunities, providing a chance to bring dreams closer to reality. The general Leo horoscope for May 2024 encourages addressing housing concerns, recognizing that waiting for a better situation may lead to prolonged delays. Taking advantage of favorable terms for obtaining a home becomes crucial during this period. With Mercury in Aries enhancing persuasion skills, Leo excels in communication, effectively establishing constructive dialogues to achieve goals.

Emotional Challenges in Love

The emotional conclusion of May introduces challenges in love. Despite the initial surge of hot dates, the future of relationships appears vague. The May horoscope recommends Leo take initiative, making bold decisions such as planning a romantic weekend to accelerate the relationship's progress. In times of unforeseen challenges, the energy of Mars in Aries provides assistance, dispelling negativity and instilling strength. Even the most indecisive Leos find renewed confidence, believing in their lucky star. Enhancing the Fire element, sitting by a lit candle or fire becomes a useful practice, harnessing cleansing and protective properties.

Additional Monthly Insights for Leo:

• Love Horoscope: The emotional conclusion of May suggests challenges in love. Taking initiative and making bold decisions, such as planning a romantic weekend, is recommended for Leo to navigate through uncertainties.

• Professional Horoscope: Perseverance fueled by the powerful Sun in Taurus opens up new opportunities for Leo. The focus on stability allows for tangible goals, and communication skills play a key role in achieving housing solutions.

- Finances: Stability graces the financial landscape in May, making goals more tangible. Leo's slightly conservative stance contributes to a positive reputation, showcasing a caring nature through gestures and words.

- Family: The Flower Full Moon heightens emotions, cautioning against touchiness. Humility is key for Leo to navigate interactions with influential individuals and maintain family harmony.

- Children: Educational conversations continue to be favored, with Mercury in Aries enhancing persuasion skills. Leo's ability to engage in constructive dialogues aids in guiding and advising effectively.

- Business: New opportunities emerge in the middle of May, providing a chance for Leo to bring dreams closer to reality. Housing solutions become a focal point, and effective communication is crucial for success.

- Money and Gains: May brings stability to the financial landscape, making goals more tangible for Leo. Opportunities to address housing concerns should be seized on favorable terms.

- Health: Caution against overstraining and undermining health, especially with the heightened emotions during the Flower Full Moon. Taking breaks and recognizing personal limits are essential for well-being.

- Astrological Aspects: The energy of Mars in Aries provides assistance in times of challenges, dispelling negativity and instilling strength. Enhancing the Fire element through practices like sitting by a lit candle or fire becomes beneficial for Leo's well-being.

June 2024 Horoscope: Leo

In June 2024, the Leo horoscope predicts the peak of business activity, offering opportunities to gain authority in professional circles and strengthen financial stability through diligence. Preparedness for increased workloads is crucial, and Leo's goodwill becomes a key asset in overcoming crisis moments. The month of Gemini fosters a spirit of contact and sincere sympathy among people, with Leo's tact earning appreciation and the acquisition of loyal allies. Leo's mood is intricately tied to external validation, making the Strawberry Full Moon in June an opportune time to boost self-esteem by focusing on skincare and hair care.

Resounding Successes in Business

The initial days of June bring resounding successes in the business sphere, with undertakings gaining approval from authorities, positively impacting funding. The Leo horoscope foresees fruitful work ahead, potentially involving collaboration with foreign colleagues. Venus in Gemini provides attractiveness and eloquence, enhancing Leo's charm and drawing others in. This presents an excellent opportunity for Leo to establish connections with influential individuals, leveraging their authority to resolve problematic issues.

Surprising Developments and Health Caution

Mid-June brings surprising developments, including long-awaited promotions, reunions with old acquaintances, or substantial bonuses. Success is anticipated in various fields, but health issues could overshadow triumphs. Leo is advised to avoid excessive alcohol and fast food. Despite the influence of Mercury in Gemini causing excitement and mood swings, Leo can maintain control over their life. While external validation was once a priority, there's a shift towards finding joy in simple pleasures, such as tidying the house and enjoying the company of guests.

Embracing Everyday Life and Family Time

Towards the end of June, more free time becomes available. The Leo horoscope recommends postponing important matters and immersing oneself in everyday life to restore strength. Switching between activities is seen as a rejuvenating practice. Mars in Taurus enhances endurance and patience, prompting Leo to prioritize a healthy lifestyle through sports and self-improvement. The shift in consciousness reflects a willingness to face challenges and embrace personal growth.

Additional Monthly Insights for Leo:

- Love Horoscope: The month of June is focused on business, but Leo's mood is influenced by external validation. The Strawberry Full Moon presents an opportunity to boost self-esteem, emphasizing skincare and hair care.

- Professional Horoscope: Business activity peaks in June, offering opportunities for authority and financial stability. Leo's goodwill and tact contribute to overcoming challenges, and collaboration with foreign colleagues is possible.

- Finances: Resounding successes in the business sphere positively impact funding in June. However, health concerns should not be overlooked, and Leo is advised to avoid excessive alcohol and fast food.

- Family: The surprising developments in mid-June may bring joy, but health issues could overshadow triumphs. Leo is encouraged to find joy in simple pleasures and prioritize a healthy lifestyle.

- Children: Leo's success in various fields in June may have positive implications for family life. Spending quality time with children and engaging in enjoyable activities contributes to a harmonious family environment.

- Business: Collaboration with foreign colleagues and the acquisition of influential allies is highlighted in June. Leo's charm and attractiveness play a crucial role in establishing valuable connections.

- Money and Gains: Success in various fields is anticipated in June, positively impacting financial stability. Leo is advised to exercise caution regarding health and avoid excesses.

- Health: Health concerns may arise in mid-June, prompting Leo to exercise caution with alcohol and dietary choices. Prioritizing a healthy lifestyle, including sports and self-improvement, becomes crucial.

- Astrological Aspects: The influence of Mars in Taurus enhances endurance and patience, contributing to Leo's ability to face challenges and embrace personal growth.

July 2024 Horoscope: Leo

In July 2024, the Leo horoscope suggests a period of slowing down and embracing a summer calm. The influence of the Sun in Cancer prompts Leo to adopt a more thoughtful approach, shifting focus towards rest and family. Prone to courageousness, Leo temporarily loses its playful mood, contemplating its role within the family. This presents an opportune time to strengthen parental authority and build trusting relationships with children. The Thunder Full Moon in July encourages self-improvement, motivating Leo to strive for perfection, both in appearance and physical fitness.

Financial Well-Being and Improved Relationships

The beginning of July brings financial well-being, offering Leo more freedom and confidence in the future. Unplanned expenses are manageable, allowing Leo to indulge in long-desired items without worry. The Leo horoscope advises seizing the opportunity to make such purchases, even if they may seem unreasonable to others. Venus in Cancer symbolizes motherly care and love, enhancing relationships with loved ones. Leo's explosive character finds the strength to compromise, fostering improved connections, particularly with parents. Taking a humble position and offering help to others can mend old grievances.

Impactful Encounters and Opportunities

Mid-July introduces new people who have a significant impact on Leo's future. Unfamiliar individuals might present enticing offers or invite Leo to a dream job. The general Leo horoscope for July 2024 emphasizes the rarity of such opportunities, urging Leo not to dismiss them. If knowledge improvement is needed, Leo is encouraged to pursue it promptly. However, the position of Mercury in Leo raises concerns about potential selfishness. Leo must be cautious not to exert undue pressure on others or impose opinions. Instead, leveraging power for benevolent purposes and helping those in need is advised.

Enchanting End of July and Health Caution

The enchanting end of July brings resolution to pending matters and the possibility of going on vacation. The Leo horoscope envisions great opportunities for relaxation, with the chance for a last-minute trip or invitations from friends to exotic destinations. Health precautions are essential, considering the position of Mars in Gemini. Leo, being naturally inclined towards winning, may overestimate the body's capabilities. Vigilance is crucial to prevent colds, as a simple runny nose could lead to complications such as sinusitis, bronchitis, or pneumonia.

Additional Monthly Insights for Leo:

• Love Horoscope: The Thunder Full Moon in July encourages self-improvement, prompting Leo to strive for perfection in appearance and physical fitness.

• Professional Horoscope: Financial well-being at the beginning of July provides confidence in the future. Seize the opportunity for unplanned expenses, and relationships with loved ones improve.

- Finances: July brings financial well-being, allowing Leo to make long-desired purchases. Improved relationships with loved ones foster a sense of stability.

- Family: Strengthening parental authority and building trusting relationships with children are highlighted in July. A humble position and offering help mend old grievances.

- Children: Improved relationships and a humble approach enhance connections with children. Educational conversations and support contribute to a harmonious family environment.

- Business: Mid-July introduces new people and opportunities that can impact Leo's future positively. Caution against selfishness and leveraging power for benevolent purposes is essential.

- Money and Gains: Financial well-being at the beginning of July provides confidence and freedom. Seizing opportunities for unplanned expenses is encouraged.

- Health: Vigilance is crucial due to the position of Mars in Gemini. Leo should be cautious not to overestimate the body's capabilities and take preventive measures against colds.

- Astrological Aspects: The enchanting end of July brings opportunities for relaxation and potential vacations. Leo is advised to be cautious about health, considering the position of Mars in Gemini.

August 2024 Horoscope: Leo

The Leo horoscope for August 2024 anticipates a spirit of adventurism, fueled by a surge of strength and energy resulting from a well-spent vacation. This increased activity is poised to have a positive impact on Leo's career, enabling success in risky projects. The month is characterized by the motto "love is above all," with Leo's natural charm significantly enhanced, attracting attention from the opposite sex. New acquaintances may evolve into exciting adventures, emphasizing the importance of being not just charming but also interesting. The Sturgeon Full Moon in August provides a developmental vector, offering numerous opportunities for growth with a defined goal.

Non-Standard Solutions and Readiness for Change

Early August presents opportunities for non-standard solutions, acting as a real lifesaver in the face of unforeseen events. The Leo horoscope suggests that being ready for change enables quick reorganization and effective action, invigorating life with a dose of unpredictability. With Venus in Virgo advocating thrift, even small purchases will be successful. Leo's strong business acumen shines as wasteful tendencies are replaced by resourcefulness. Capable hands can bring new life to outdated items, making it an opportune time for housecleaning and repairs on a budget.

Joyful Events and Financial Caution

The middle of August brings joyous events and memorable meetings, but the Leo horoscope warns of a potentially tense financial situation. Creative approaches, such as organizing cost-effective field trips instead of restaurant gatherings, can help navigate financial challenges. The position of Mercury in Leo, signaling potential selfishness, underscores the importance of using power for benevolent purposes. Leo is encouraged to help those in need rather than imposing opinions on others.

Teamwork and Official Chores

The last days of August involve running around and handling official chores, but they don't guarantee quick career advancement; it's circumstantial. The Leo horoscope recommends betting on teamwork, as colleagues can provide crucial support in critical moments and, if successful, help organize a celebration. Health precautions are vital due to the position of Mars in Gemini. Leo's natural inclination to overestimate the body's capabilities requires extra vigilance. Preventive measures against colds are essential to avoid complications like sinusitis, bronchitis, or pneumonia.

Additional Monthly Insights for Leo:

• Love Horoscope: The enhanced charm of Leo attracts the attention of the opposite sex. New acquaintances may turn into exciting adventures, emphasizing the importance of being interesting beyond charm.

• Professional Horoscope: Increased activity in August positively impacts Leo's career, facilitating success in risky projects. The Sturgeon Full Moon provides a developmental vector with numerous growth opportunities.

- Finances: Thriftiness, encouraged by Venus in Virgo, contributes to successful small purchases. Leo's business acumen shines as resourcefulness replaces wasteful tendencies.

- Family: Non-standard solutions and readiness for change invigorate family life. Housecleaning and repairs can be undertaken with minimal funds.

- Children: Joyful events and memorable meetings in mid-August may involve certain costs. Creative approaches can help navigate potential financial challenges.

- Business: Teamwork is recommended in the last days of August, with colleagues providing crucial support. Health precautions are essential due to the position of Mars in Gemini.

- Money and Gains: Tense financial situations in mid-August require creative approaches. Leo is encouraged to be thrifty and consider cost-effective alternatives.

- Health: Vigilance is crucial against potential health issues, especially considering Leo's tendency to overestimate the body's capabilities. Preventive measures against colds are essential.

September 2024 Horoscope: Leo

The Leo horoscope for September 2024 ushers in a whirlwind of emotions as autumn begins. Love takes center stage, bringing both passion and potential conflicts. The Sun in Virgo highlights a practical approach to relationships, emphasizing communication and understanding. Amidst the Harvest Full Moon's influence, emotions run high, requiring careful navigation to maintain balance. Patience and a level-headed approach will be key to avoiding unnecessary disputes.

First Days of September - Financial Well-being:

The month kicks off with a stable financial outlook for Leo. It's an opportune time to review and plan expenses wisely. Unexpected windfalls may provide additional resources, allowing Leos to indulge in some desired but reasonable purchases. However, caution is advised to ensure long-term financial stability.

Middle of September - Impactful New Connections:

Mid-September brings exciting opportunities for new connections. Networking efforts can lead to beneficial collaborations both personally and professionally. The general Leo horoscope for this period suggests being open to diverse interactions. Leverage these connections for personal growth and potential career advancements.

End of September - Vibrant Impressions and Health Caution:

As September concludes, vibrant impressions and experiences mark this period. Leo will find joy in social activities and may receive recognition for their creative endeavors. However, amidst the excitement, health caution is paramount. With Mars in Cancer, it's crucial for Leo to prioritize self-care, ensuring physical well-being amid the festivities.

Additional Monthly Insights for Leo:

- **Love** Horoscope: The month encourages open communication in relationships. Leos may face passionate moments, and addressing concerns with a level-headed approach fosters understanding.

- **Professional** Horoscope: Career growth opportunities arise, but careful consideration is needed before making significant decisions. Leverage newfound connections for a positive impact on professional endeavors.

- Finances: Prudent financial planning is advised, especially considering potential unexpected expenses. A balance between indulgence and fiscal responsibility is key for Leo's financial well-being.

- Family: Family dynamics may experience shifts. Active efforts to maintain harmony are crucial, and open communication helps resolve any tensions that may arise.

- Children: Quality time with children is emphasized. Paying attention to their emotional needs strengthens the parent-child bond.

- Business: Entrepreneurial ventures may see positive developments. Collaborations and partnerships formed in September contribute to long-term success.

- Money and Gains: Flexibility and adaptability in financial matters are highlighted. Leo's ability to navigate challenges with optimism contributes to overall financial stability.

- Health: Vigilance against potential health issues is crucial, especially focusing on stress management and maintaining a balanced lifestyle.

- Astrological Aspects: Pluto's alignment underscores the importance of transformative experiences. The eclipse in September signifies a period of culmination and personal growth for Leo.

October 2024 Horoscope: Leo

According to the Leo horoscope, October 2024 ushers in a period of exceptional luck and positive changes. A wind of transformation sweeps through life, bringing forth opportunities for career growth, increased income, and enhanced respect in professional circles. The month of Libra emphasizes harmony, making it an ideal time for creative endeavors, including home improvement projects. The Hunter's Full Moon in October signals a pivotal moment for Leo, where bold ideas manifest into reality, and leadership recognizes and rewards Leo's professionalism.

Early October - Embracing Change and Career Growth:

At the start of October, a sense of stagnation may be felt in work. The Leo horoscope recommends injecting novelty into the routine to reignite passion. Individual coaching can broaden professional horizons. Venus in Scorpio contributes to positive transformations, and visualization meditation enhances self-esteem, fostering a belief in a bright future.

Middle of October - Strategic Risk-Taking and Analytical Skills:

Mid-October favors those willing to take calculated risks. While impulsive influences from Mercury in Scorpio may arise, Leo's analytical skills should guide decision-making. Careful consideration and strategic thinking will minimize the risk of conflicts and maintain a smooth course. Balancing risk and security measures is key for success.

End of October - Fulfillment of Dreams and Prosperity:

The month concludes with a remarkable period, hinting at the fulfillment of long-held dreams. The October horoscope for Leo foresees prosperity unfolding seamlessly. Success comes effortlessly, and dreams such as weddings, childbirth, or homeownership may materialize. Despite potential challenges due to Mars in Cancer, maintaining an energy-saving mode and embracing yoga can ensure inner balance.

Additional Monthly Insights for Leo:

- Love Horoscope: A fortunate time for romantic relationships. Leos may experience positive developments, and passionate connections may lead to significant milestones.

- Professional Horoscope: Career shifts are notable, especially during the Hunter's Full Moon. Recognition of Leo's capabilities and bold initiatives propels professional advancement.

- Finances: Financial stability prevails, but Leo should remain vigilant against impulsive spending. Wise financial planning ensures long-term prosperity.

- Family: The supportive atmosphere contributes to family harmony. Open communication helps navigate any potential conflicts that may arise.

- Children: Quality time spent with children is emphasized, strengthening the parent-child bond. Leo's guidance positively influences their children's well-being.

- Business: Entrepreneurial ventures thrive, and calculated risks lead to positive outcomes. Leo's strategic decisions contribute to the success of business endeavors.

- Money and Gains: A period of financial ease and minimal extra costs. Leo's adaptability ensures financial stability, even in the face of potential challenges.

- Health: Maintaining an energy-saving mode is crucial for well-being. Incorporating yoga into the routine helps Leo achieve balance and tranquility.

- Astrological Aspects: Mars in Cancer may introduce challenges, emphasizing the need for a measured approach. The impact of Mars can be mitigated through mindful energy management and holistic practices like yoga.

November 2024 Horoscope: Leo

The Leo horoscope for November 2023 advises a focus on meaningful connections and avoiding unnecessary distractions. As cold weather sets in, addressing the need for love becomes crucial. Instead of dwelling on relationship conflicts, emphasis should be on strengthening family bonds. The potent influence of the Sun in Scorpio heightens attraction, but caution is advised to avoid impulsive actions. Family-oriented Leos may face tests of loyalty, necessitating self-control to prevent betrayals. The Beaver Full Moon in November underscores the importance of building a solid foundation with trustworthy allies before pursuing career aspirations.

Early November - Relationship Caution and Family Focus:

With the Sun in Scorpio, early November calls for restraint in relationships. Family ties should take precedence, and passion should be tempered to avoid betrayals. The Beaver Full Moon guides Leo to establish a reliable support network before venturing into ambitious career goals.

Middle of November - Tense Communication and Thrifty Ventures:

The initial days bring tension to communication, prompting a brief period of seclusion. However, the Leo horoscope assures a positive shift soon. The influence of Venus in Virgo favors wise financial decisions, urging Leos to be thrifty. Successful ventures with minimal expenses and creative refurbishments are encouraged.

End of November - Career Projects and Social Significance:

The middle of the month sees a positive turn, aligning Leo with profitable projects. Though success may take time, participation in lucrative endeavors is promising. Despite potential friction with authorities, maintaining confidence and belief in one's abilities is crucial. Under Mercury in Sagittarius, irrational thinking should be kept in check to avoid distorted perceptions.

Calm End of November - Stability and Adventure:

The calm end of November brings resolution to conflicts, stabilizing the overall situation. According to the November horoscope for Leo, life is viewed as a grand adventure. Self-confidence grows, attracting a supportive community. While Mars in Scorpio encourages risk-taking, maintaining a balance between thrill-seeking and practicality is vital to prevent health issues.

Additional Monthly Insights for Leo:

• Love Horoscope: Caution in romantic relationships is advised to prevent impulsive actions. Family bonds take precedence, and loyalty is key to maintaining harmony.

• Professional Horoscope: Building a reliable support network is essential before pursuing ambitious career goals. The middle of November presents opportunities for participation in profitable projects.

- Finances: Thrifty financial decisions are favored, ensuring successful ventures with minimal expenses. Creative refurbishments at home contribute to a sense of financial prudence.

- Family: Prioritizing family ties and addressing conflicts positively impact overall well-being. The supportive atmosphere aids in navigating challenges.

- Children: Quality time with children strengthens the parent-child bond. Balanced attention to their needs contributes to a harmonious family life.

- Business: Despite potential challenges, participating in profitable projects is promising. Confidence and belief in personal abilities contribute to success.

- Money and Gains: Wise financial decisions lead to financial stability. Leos' adaptability ensures minimal financial losses and a sense of security.

- Health: Balancing thrill-seeking with practicality is crucial to prevent health issues. Attention to clothing for weather protection is emphasized to avoid chronic diseases.

Astrological Aspects:

Mars in Cancer may introduce challenges, emphasizing the need for a measured approach. The impact of Mars can be mitigated through mindful energy management and holistic practices like yoga.

December 2024 Horoscope: Leo

The Leo horoscope for December 2023 promises a vibrant conclusion to the year, marked by financial stability and opportunities for personal growth. As the financial situation stabilizes, indulging in luxuries becomes feasible, making it an ideal time for a rejuvenating vacation to uplift spirits and showcase status. The Sun in Sagittarius inspires a desire for life changes and increased harmony, urging Leo to tap into intuition for a more fulfilling existence. Business success becomes a compensatory factor for any setbacks in other areas, reaching its peak during the Cold Full Moon in December, providing a favorable period for transactions and negotiations.

Early December - Financial Stability and Intuitive Guidance:

Financial stability characterizes early December, presenting a dual challenge of a steady income flow and the temptation for extravagant spending. The Leo horoscope advises moderation, cautioning against financial recklessness. Instead, leveraging resources for business development is recommended. Venus in Libra encourages an appreciation of beauty, offering an opportunity for creative pursuits and the discovery of latent talents.

Middle of December - Career Changes and Societal Success:

The middle of the month brings potential career changes, accompanied by new connections and increased income. These developments reflect the fruits of a well-executed career strategy, allowing Leo to revel in deserved accomplishments. The general Leo horoscope for December 2023 propels individuals into a new sphere, adorned with societal status and the trappings of a successful business person. Minimal losses are ensured by the influence of Mercury in Capricorn, offering a steady hand in navigating challenges.

Last Days of December - Pre-Holiday Bustle and Family Involvement:

The concluding days of December unfold in a flurry of pre-holiday activities, marked by numerous meetings, new acquaintances, and gift exchanges. The December horoscope for Leo suggests active family involvement, recognizing that work becomes more enjoyable and efficient in good company. With Mars in Sagittarius providing momentum to ideas, Leos find it easier to bring tasks to completion. Despite potential competition, Leos stand firm, demonstrating resilience and determination. Balancing the festive bustle, periodic retreats for self-reflection and energy conservation practices are recommended to maintain inner equilibrium.

Additional Monthly Insights for Leo:

- Love Horoscope: The emphasis on financial stability allows for enjoyable romantic experiences. Caution in spending ensures long-term stability in relationships.

- Professional Horoscope: Career changes bring new opportunities, increasing income and societal recognition. A well-thought-out career strategy yields deserved success.

- Finances: Financial stability prevails, but caution in spending is essential. Utilizing resources for business development and creative pursuits is advisable.

- Family: Active family involvement enhances the festive atmosphere. Quality time spent together contributes to a harmonious end to the year.

- Children: Involving children in holiday activities strengthens familial bonds. Balancing festivities with moments of calm aids in their overall well-being.

- Business: Career changes result in increased income and societal status. The ability to navigate challenges with minimal losses ensures a successful transition.

- Money and Gains: Financial stability allows for indulgences, but strategic spending is crucial. Leos' adaptability ensures minimal financial losses and a sense of security.

- Health: Amidst the holiday bustle, periodic retreats for self-reflection and energy conservation practices are vital for maintaining overall well-being.

Astrological Aspects:

Mars in Sagittarius provides momentum to ideas and tasks, facilitating their successful completion. Energy conservation practices are recommended to balance the festive activities.

Astrological Remedies

Leo's individuals can benefit from specific astrological remedies in 2024 to enhance their overall well-being and address challenges. Here are some remedies that can be helpful:

1. Wear Ruby Gemstone: The ruby is the birthstone for Leos and is associated with the Sun. Wearing a natural and high-quality ruby gemstone can enhance your energy, confidence, and leadership qualities. It's believed to bring positive changes in various aspects of life.

2. Chant the Sun Mantra: Recite the "Om Suryaya Namaha" mantra daily. This mantra is dedicated to the Sun, your ruling planet. Chanting it can strengthen your connection with the Sun and its positive influences in your life.

3. Perform Surya Namaskar: Incorporate the practice of Surya Namaskar (Sun Salutation) into your daily routine. This yoga sequence is a way to pay homage to the Sun and helps in maintaining physical and mental health.

4. Donate to Charities: Making regular donations to charities and participating in acts of kindness can help balance any negative energies and promote positivity in your life.

5. Worship Lord Shiva: Leo individuals can also benefit from worshiping Lord Shiva. Offer water and milk to the Shivling and recite Shiva mantras to seek blessings for harmony and balance in life.

6. Seek the Blessings of the Sun: Every Sunday, offer water and red flowers to the Sun god. This simple ritual can help strengthen your connection with the Sun, enhancing its positive influence on your life.

These astrological remedies can help Leo individuals navigate the challenges and maximize the opportunities that 2024 has in store. It's essential to practice them with sincerity and faith for the best results.

Frequently Asked Questions:

1. How will the year 2024 be for Leo natives?

o The year 2024 holds the promise of financial stability and opportunities for Leo individuals.

2. What is the business horoscope for Leo in 2024?

o In 2024, Leos will be actively seeking new opportunities to enhance their personal and financial growth in the business sector.

3. What is the career outlook for Leo in 2024?

o Leo individuals have a higher likelihood of receiving promotions and advancing in their careers during 2024.

4. Which zodiac signs are compatible with Leo?

o Leo is most compatible with other fire signs, such as Aries, Leo, and Sagittarius, who share their enthusiasm and energy.

5. Is 2024 lucky for Leo?

o Yes, 2024 is expected to bring favorable circumstances and opportunities for Leo natives, making it a lucky year for them.

LEO: THE LION

Leo, the fifth sign of the zodiac, is symbolized by the majestic lion. Those born under this sign typically fall between July 23rd and August 22nd. Leo is ruled by the Sun, and much like the Sun is the center of our solar system, Leos often find themselves at the center of attention due to their vibrant personalities and charismatic presence.

Characteristics of Leo:

1. Confidence: Leos are known for their unwavering self-confidence. They exude an air of self-assuredness and carry themselves with a regal and dignified demeanor. This confidence is one of their most defining traits.

2. Generosity: Leo is a sign associated with generosity. Leos have big hearts and a willingness to give to others. They are often the first to help a friend in need or support a charitable cause.

3. Leadership: Natural leaders, Leos have a strong desire to take charge of situations. They thrive in positions of authority and are often the go-to person for guidance and decision-making.

4. Charisma: Leos possess a magnetic charm that draws people toward them. Their charisma is a key factor in their ability to influence and lead others effectively.

5. Creativity: Creativity flows through Leos, and they often have a strong artistic streak. They enjoy expressing themselves through various forms of art, be it music, painting, or performing arts.

6. Passion: Leos are intensely passionate individuals. They approach life with enthusiasm and zeal, which makes them stand out in whatever they pursue.

7. Determination: Once a Leo sets their mind on a goal, they pursue it with unwavering determination. Their persistence is admirable and often leads to successful outcomes.

8. Courage: The lion is known for its courage, and this trait is mirrored in Leos. They face challenges head-on and are not easily deterred by obstacles.

9. Optimism: Leos have a sunny disposition and tend to see the glass as half full. Their positivity is infectious and can uplift the spirits of those around them.

10. Loyalty: Loyalty is of utmost importance to Leos. They are fiercely loyal to their friends and loved ones, often going to great lengths to support and protect them.

Personality Traits of Leo:

· Extroverted: Leos are extroverts by nature. They thrive in social settings and enjoy being the center of attention. Their outgoing personalities make them natural entertainers and great company.

· Energetic: Full of vitality, Leos have an abundance of energy. They approach life with gusto and are always ready to take on new challenges.

· Ego: While their confidence is a strength, it can sometimes manifest as a larger-than-life ego. Leos must be mindful of becoming overly self-centered or arrogant.

· Dramatic: Leos have a flair for the dramatic. They enjoy theatrics and often bring an element of grandeur to their daily lives.

· Attention-Seeking: Leos have a strong desire to be recognized and admired. They appreciate compliments and recognition for their achievements.

Significance of Leo:

Leo is a fire sign, and like a roaring fire, Leos are known for their warmth and passion. They are natural leaders who bring vitality and a sense of purpose to their endeavors. In the grand tapestry of the zodiac, Leo holds a special place as the sign associated with creativity and self-expression.

Leos are often drawn to careers in the arts, entertainment, and leadership roles. They excel as actors, musicians, politicians, and entrepreneurs. Their charisma and ability to captivate an audience make them ideal for positions that require public speaking or performance.

In relationships, Leos are loyal and passionate partners. They seek a deep emotional connection and enjoy showering their loved ones with affection and gifts. However, they also require admiration and recognition from their partners.

In conclusion, Leo, the lion of the zodiac, represents confidence, generosity, leadership, and a flair for the dramatic. Leos are known for their charisma and their ability to light up any room they enter. Their creative spirit and determination make them stand out in their pursuits. This marks the end of our overview of Leo, and if you'd like to explore specific aspects of Leo's personality or their compatibility with other zodiac signs, please let me know.

Confidence is one of the most striking characteristics of Leo individuals. Leos are known for their unwavering self-assuredness and a strong belief in their abilities. They exude a natural sense of confidence that often sets them apart from others. This self-assuredness is deeply rooted in Leo's ruling celestial body, the Sun, which radiates warmth and vitality.

Leos have a remarkable ability to tackle challenges with a positive outlook and a belief in their own competence. They are not easily swayed by self-doubt and are more likely to embrace opportunities with open arms. This self-confidence makes them natural leaders and influencers in various aspects of life.

Leo's confidence is often evident in the way they carry themselves. They have a regal and dignified demeanor that reflects their self-assured nature. This air of authority can be magnetic, drawing others to them and making them the center of attention in social settings.

However, it's important to note that while confidence is a remarkable trait, it can sometimes manifest as a larger-than-life ego in Leo individuals. They should be mindful of striking a balance between self-assuredness and humility to maintain harmonious relationships with others.

In relationships, Leo's confidence can translate into being a strong and supportive partner. They often offer unwavering emotional support and are known for being the rock in their relationships. Their confidence can be reassuring to their loved ones, making them feel secure and protected.

In professional settings, Leo's confidence is an asset. They excel in leadership roles and are often seen at the helm of projects and teams. Their ability to make decisive decisions and lead with conviction is highly valued by colleagues and superiors.

In summary, confidence is a fundamental trait of Leo individuals. It is deeply intertwined with their personality, making them natural leaders, influencers, and sources of support in both personal and professional relationships. As we continue generating content, we'll explore other significant aspects of Leo's character and their compatibility with other zodiac signs.

GENEROSITY:

Generosity is another prominent trait in Leo individuals. Those born under this zodiac sign are known for their big hearts and their willingness to give to others. They possess a genuine and benevolent nature that shines through in their actions and interactions with people around them.

Leos are generous in various ways, be it with their time, resources, or emotional support. They often go the extra mile to help friends, family, and even strangers in need. Their innate sense of kindness and compassion makes them reliable sources of support and comfort for those around them.

One of the significant ways in which Leos express their generosity is through their ability to uplift the spirits of others. They have a knack for brightening up a room with their warm presence and lively energy. Their contagious positivity is like a beacon of hope, especially during challenging times.

In relationships, Leo's generosity is highly appreciated by their partners. They are known for pampering their loved ones with thoughtful gestures, gifts, and acts of love. Leos thrive on making their partners feel special and cherished. They are also fiercely loyal, which is another way they express their generosity in relationships.

Leos often involve themselves in charitable work and community service. Their desire to make a positive impact on the world leads them to support various causes and organizations. Whether it's volunteering, donating, or organizing events, Leos are actively involved in making the world a better place.

However, it's worth noting that Leo's generosity can sometimes be taken advantage of by individuals who may not have the best intentions. Their willingness to help and their open-hearted nature can leave them vulnerable to those who may seek to exploit their kindness.

In the professional world, Leos' generosity can be seen in their willingness to mentor and support colleagues. They are often found in leadership roles where they can make decisions that benefit the team as a whole. Their generosity extends to sharing their knowledge and helping others succeed.

In conclusion, generosity is a central characteristic of Leo individuals. Their open-hearted and giving nature sets them apart as people who genuinely care about the well-being of those around them. As we continue generating content, we'll explore other facets of Leo's personality and delve deeper into their significance in the zodiac.

Leadership:

Leadership is a defining trait of Leo individuals. They are natural-born leaders, driven by a deep desire to take charge of situations and guide others toward success. The lion, which represents Leo, is often seen as the king of the animal kingdom, and this symbolism is reflected in the way Leos approach leadership.

Leos have an innate ability to inspire and motivate those around them. They lead by example and are often the go-to person when important decisions need to be made. Their self-confidence and charisma make them effective leaders who can rally people behind a cause or a project.

In both personal and professional settings, Leo individuals are drawn to leadership roles. They have a natural magnetism that draws people towards them, and this is a key factor in their ability to influence and lead effectively. They thrive in positions of authority and are unafraid of shouldering the responsibilities that come with leadership.

One of the remarkable aspects of Leo's leadership style is their unwavering determination. When they set their sights on a goal, they pursue it with relentless commitment. Their persistence and belief in their abilities often lead to successful outcomes, making them respected figures in their chosen fields.

In the workplace, Leo individuals are often seen as the driving force behind projects and teams. They are not afraid to make tough decisions, and their decisiveness is appreciated by colleagues and superiors. Leos excel in roles that require them to take the lead, whether it's as managers, entrepreneurs, or in any position that demands authority.

In relationships, Leo's leadership qualities can be both reassuring and inspiring. They are protective and devoted partners who often take on the role of the provider and the decisionmaker. Their partners appreciate their strong and dependable nature.

However, it's important for Leo individuals to strike a balance between their leadership and allowing others to have their voices heard. Their confidence and desire to take charge can sometimes come across as dominating, which may lead to conflicts in personal and professional relationships.

In conclusion, leadership is a central aspect of Leo's personality. They are natural leaders who inspire, motivate, and take charge of situations with unwavering determination. As we continue generating content, we'll explore other key traits and characteristics of Leo, as well as their compatibility with other zodiac signs.

Creativity:

Creativity is a vibrant and essential aspect of Leo individuals. They possess an innate artistic streak that sets them apart from other zodiac signs. Leo's creativity is fueled by their passion, enthusiasm, and their desire to express themselves in unique and imaginative ways.

Leo's association with creativity is in harmony with their ruling celestial body, the Sun. This connection reflects the light, warmth, and vitality that Leo individuals bring into the world. They have a natural ability to infuse their creativity into everything they do.

One of the most common ways Leo expresses their creativity is through the arts. They have a profound appreciation for music, painting, theater, and other forms of artistic expression. Many famous musicians, actors, and artists are born under the Leo sign, which is a testament to their creative abilities.

Leo individuals are not just consumers of art; they are often creators themselves. They have a deep-seated desire to produce beautiful and meaningful work. Their artistic endeavors are driven by their passion for self-expression and a need to share their unique perspectives with the world.

Their creative flair extends to their approach to problem-solving. Leos often come up with innovative and imaginative solutions to challenges. They think outside the box and are unafraid to take risks, which can lead to breakthroughs in various fields.

Leos are known for their dramatic and theatrical tendencies. They enjoy creating experiences that are larger than life and filled with excitement. This love for theatrics can be seen in their social interactions, events they organize, and their natural ability to captivate an audience.

In relationships, Leo's creativity shines through in their romantic gestures. They have a knack for planning unforgettable dates and surprising their partners with thoughtful gifts. Their creativity adds an element of excitement and passion to their love lives.

In the professional world, Leo's creative energy can lead them to careers in the arts, entertainment, and design.

They excel in fields where their imaginative thinking and artistic talents can be fully expressed.

However, it's important to note that Leo's creativity can sometimes be accompanied by a desire for recognition and admiration. They appreciate when others acknowledge their creative efforts and talents, which can lead to a need for validation.

In conclusion, creativity is a fundamental trait of Leo individuals. They possess a deep appreciation for the arts and have a natural talent for self-expression and innovation. Their creative energy adds vibrancy and excitement to their lives and the lives of those around them. As we continue generating content, we'll explore more aspects of Leo's personality and delve into their compatibility with other zodiac signs.

Passion:

Passion is at the core of Leo individuals' personalities. Those born under this zodiac sign approach life with an unparalleled enthusiasm and a zeal for everything they do. This deep-seated passion is one of the key factors that make Leos stand out in the world of the zodiac.

Leos are known for their intensity, whether it's in pursuing their goals, engaging in hobbies, or nurturing their relationships. Their enthusiasm is infectious and can inspire those around them to embrace life with similar fervor.

One of the most remarkable aspects of Leo's passion is their commitment to their dreams and aspirations. When they set their sights on a goal, they pursue it with unwavering dedication. Their determination, combined with their fiery spirit, often leads to remarkable achievements in various aspects of life.

In personal relationships, Leo's passion manifests as an unwavering devotion to their loved ones. They invest a tremendous amount of emotional energy into their relationships, making them loving and loyal partners. Their intense love and affection are evident in the way they pamper and protect those they care about.

Leo's passion extends to their interests and hobbies. They have a natural ability to immerse themselves fully in their chosen pursuits, whether it's a sport, a creative project, or a cause they believe in. This passion often leads to excellence in their endeavors.

In the professional world, Leo individuals bring their passion to their careers. They are often motivated by a desire to make a meaningful impact in their chosen field. Their enthusiasm and drive can lead to successful careers in leadership, entrepreneurship, and creative industries.

However, it's important to note that Leo's passion can sometimes border on stubbornness. When they are deeply committed to a course of action, they may be resistant to change or compromise. This determination, while a strength, can also lead to conflicts if not managed effectively.

In conclusion, passion is a defining characteristic of Leo individuals. Their intense enthusiasm and unwavering commitment set them apart as people who approach life with fervor and dedication. As we continue generating content, we'll explore other significant aspects of Leo's personality and their compatibility with other zodiac signs.

Determination:

Determination is a hallmark trait of Leo individuals. Once they set their minds on a goal, they pursue it with unyielding resolve and tenacity. Their determination is often seen as a driving force that propels them toward success in various aspects of life.

Leos possess a unique combination of confidence, passion, and perseverance. When faced with challenges or obstacles, they don't easily back down. Instead, they confront these challenges head-on, displaying a remarkable level of inner strength.

One of the key aspects of Leo's determination is their unwavering belief in their abilities. They trust in their competence and have a "can-do" attitude that allows them to tackle even the most daunting tasks with optimism. Their positive outlook and self-assuredness are sources of inspiration for those around them.

In personal relationships, Leo's determination is a source of reliability and support. They are the ones you can count on in times of need, always ready to offer a helping hand or a listening ear. Their loyalty to their friends and loved ones is unwavering.

In the professional world, Leos excel in roles that demand leadership and decisiveness. Their determination to succeed often leads them to positions of authority where they can make impactful decisions. They are not easily discouraged by setbacks, which is a quality highly valued by colleagues and superiors.

Leo's determination also extends to their pursuit of creative endeavors. Whether it's in the arts or other creative fields, they exhibit a relentless drive to express themselves and produce meaningful work. Their creative projects often benefit from their dedication and persistence.

However, it's important to acknowledge that Leo's determination can sometimes lead to stubbornness. Their unwavering commitment to their goals may make them resistant to change or alternative approaches. Learning to balance their determination with flexibility is essential for maintaining harmonious relationships.

In conclusion, determination is a central feature of Leo individuals. Their unrelenting resolve and self-confidence make them formidable in their pursuits, whether in personal relationships, creative endeavors, or their careers. As we continue generating content, we'll explore other dimensions of Leo's personality and their compatibility with other zodiac signs.

Courage:

Courage is a key trait that defines Leo individuals. Like the lion, their zodiac symbol, Leos possess a fearless and bold disposition. They face challenges with bravery and determination, making them stand out as individuals who are unafraid to confront life's obstacles.

Leos are not easily deterred by adversity. Instead, they tackle difficulties head-on, displaying a remarkable level of inner strength. This courage is closely linked to their self-confidence and unwavering belief in their abilities.

One of the most notable aspects of Leo's courage is their ability to take calculated risks. They are not afraid to step outside their comfort zones and embrace new opportunities, even when there is uncertainty involved. This willingness to take risks often leads to significant achievements and personal growth.

In personal relationships, Leo's courage can be a source of inspiration and support for their loved ones. They are often the ones who stand up for their friends and family when faced with challenges or injustices. Their protective nature and willingness to defend those they care about are evident in their actions.

In the professional world, Leos are often drawn to positions that require bravery and leadership. They are unafraid to make tough decisions and take on challenging projects. Their courage in the face of adversity often leads to successful outcomes and advancements in their careers.

Leo's courage also extends to their creative pursuits. They are not afraid to express themselves artistically and share their work with the world. Their willingness to put themselves out there and take risks in creative endeavors often leads to recognition and success.

However, it's important to note that Leo's courage can sometimes be accompanied by a tendency to be overly competitive or domineering. Their fearless nature may lead to conflicts if not balanced with humility and consideration for others' viewpoints.

In conclusion, courage is a fundamental trait of Leo individuals. Their fearless disposition and willingness to confront challenges head-on make them admirable and impactful in various aspects of life. As we continue generating content, we'll explore other significant aspects of Leo's personality and their compatibility with other zodiac signs.

Optimism:

Optimism is a radiant and defining trait of Leo individuals. They possess a sunny disposition and tend to see the world through a positive lens. Their natural enthusiasm and hopefulness bring light and warmth to their interactions and endeavors.

Leos approach life with a "glass half full" mentality. Their positivity is not just a superficial outlook; it's a fundamental part of their character. This optimism is often a source of inspiration for those around them, as it encourages a brighter outlook on life.

One of the most remarkable aspects of Leo's optimism is their ability to uplift the spirits of others. They have a magnetic personality that attracts people to them, and their positive energy is contagious. In challenging times, they serve as beacons of hope, reminding those around them that there is always a silver lining.

In personal relationships, Leo's optimism is highly appreciated by their loved ones. They provide unwavering emotional support and encouragement, helping their partners and friends navigate life's ups and downs with a positive attitude. Their optimism often acts as a stabilizing force in relationships.

In the professional world, Leos' optimism is a valuable asset. They approach their work with enthusiasm and are known for their ability to inspire colleagues. Their positive outlook on challenges and the future often leads to increased morale and productivity in the workplace.

Leo's optimism also extends to their creative endeavors. They are not afraid to embrace new artistic challenges and are driven by a belief in the power of creativity to make the world a better place. Their hopefulness often leads to innovative and meaningful contributions to the arts.

However, it's important to acknowledge that Leo's optimism can sometimes be taken to an extreme, leading to a tendency to overlook challenges or underestimate the effort required for certain tasks. Maintaining a balance between optimism and realistic expectations is crucial for achieving success.

In conclusion, optimism is a central feature of Leo individuals. Their positivity and hopefulness set them apart as individuals who radiate light and warmth, making them sources of inspiration and support for those around them. As we continue generating content, we'll explore other significant aspects of Leo's personality and their compatibility with other zodiac signs.

Loyalty:

Loyalty is a core characteristic of Leo individuals. They place a high value on their relationships, whether they are with friends, family, or romantic partners. When a Leo commits to a bond, they do so with unwavering dedication and devotion.

One of the most striking aspects of Leo's loyalty is their fierce commitment to their loved ones. They stand by their friends and family through thick and thin, providing unwavering support and protection. Leo is the friend you can count on in times of need and the family member who will always be there.

In romantic relationships, Leo's loyalty is deeply significant. They are known for being faithful and dedicated partners who prioritize their loved ones above all else. Their passion and enthusiasm are channeled into their relationships, making them loving and affectionate partners.

Leo individuals are not only loyal but also fiercely protective. They take it upon themselves to shield their loved ones from harm and provide a sense of security. This protective nature often comes across as a strong and reliable support system.

In the professional world, Leo's loyalty is reflected in their commitment to their work and colleagues. They are known for being team players who support their coworkers and contribute to the success of their organizations. Their loyalty often leads to lasting and valuable professional relationships.

Leo's loyalty is not limited to personal and professional relationships; it extends to their values and beliefs. They are dedicated to causes and principles they hold dear and are often involved in charitable work and community service. Their desire to make a positive impact on the world is a testament to their loyalty to broader societal goals.

However, it's important to acknowledge that Leo's loyalty can sometimes lead to possessiveness or a tendency to be overly protective, which may strain relationships. Finding a balance between loyalty and allowing freedom and independence for their loved ones is essential for maintaining healthy and harmonious relationships.

In conclusion, loyalty is a fundamental trait of Leo individuals. Their unwavering dedication and protective nature make them cherished and reliable friends, family members, and partners.

Turn-ons

That are often associated with Leo individuals:

1. Admiration and Recognition: Leos are known for their desire to be admired and recognized for their achievements. Offering genuine compliments and acknowledging their talents and efforts can be a significant turn-on for them.

2. Attention: Leo individuals enjoy being the center of attention. They are often drawn to partners who appreciate their charismatic and confident presence and who give them undivided attention.

3. Passion: Leos are intensely passionate individuals, and they are attracted to partners who share their zeal for life. Embracing their enthusiasm and joining them in pursuing shared interests can be a major turn-on.

4. Loyalty: Loyalty is a core value for Leo, so they appreciate partners who are equally devoted and loyal. Demonstrating your commitment to the relationship can be very attractive to Leo.

5. Creative Expression: Leos have a strong creative streak, so they are often drawn to partners who appreciate and encourage their artistic endeavors. Participating in creative activities together can be a turn-on for Leo.

6. Confidence: Leo's confidence is a key trait, and they are often attracted to partners who exude selfassuredness. Confidence can create a magnetic

attraction for Leo individuals.

7. Generosity: Leo values generosity and kindness. Acts of generosity and thoughtfulness, such as surprising them with thoughtful gifts or gestures, can be quite appealing to Leo.

8. Playfulness: Leos often enjoy a good sense of humor and playfulness. Light-hearted and fun interactions with a partner can be a turn-on for Leo.

9. Support: Being supportive and encouraging of Leo's goals and ambitions is highly attractive. Leo appreciates a partner who stands by their side and believes in their abilities.

10. Romantic Gestures: Leo is known for their romantic nature. Thoughtful and romantic gestures, such as surprise dates, love letters, or creating special moments, can be significant turn-ons.

Remember that individual preferences can vary, and not all Leos are the same. It's essential to communicate openly with your Leo partner to understand their specific desires and turnons in your relationship.

Turn-offs

That may be associated with Leo individuals

1. EGO-CRUSHING CRITICISM: One of the significant turn-offs for Leo individuals is harsh and ego-crushing criticism. Leos have a strong sense of self-confidence and take pride in their abilities and achievements. When their partners or peers constantly criticize or belittle them, it can be extremely disheartening for Leo. They value constructive feedback and support but detest being made to feel inferior or inadequate. In relationships, it's crucial to balance criticism with encouragement and positivity to avoid dampening Leo's spirits.

2. Lack of Appreciation: Leos thrive on admiration and appreciation. They enjoy being recognized for their efforts and the value they bring to their relationships and endeavors. A significant turn-off for Leo is feeling unappreciated or taken for granted. If their contributions, whether in a relationship or at work, go unnoticed or unacknowledged, it can lead to feelings of disappointment and frustration. To keep Leo engaged and happy, it's essential to express gratitude and regularly acknowledge their accomplishments.

3. Negativity and Pessimism: Leo individuals are naturally optimistic and have a sunny disposition. They are attracted to positivity and enthusiasm in others. What can

be a major turn-off for Leo is a consistently negative and pessimistic attitude from their partners or those around them. Constantly dwelling on problems, complaining, or being excessively cynical can drain Leo's energy and enthusiasm. They are more drawn to individuals who share their optimism and can uplift their spirits.

4. Dominance and Control: While Leos appreciate a partner who can take the lead, they also value their independence and autonomy. Being overly dominant, controlling, or possessive in a relationship can be a significant turn-off for Leo. They thrive in partnerships that offer a sense of equality and freedom. Excessive control can lead to feelings of suffocation, which is contrary to Leo's desire for space and self-expression.

5. Lack of Support and Encouragement: Leo individuals are highly supportive of their loved ones, and they expect the same in return. One of the major turn-offs for Leo is a lack of support and encouragement from their partners or friends. Feeling like their dreams, goals, or creative pursuits are not valued or endorsed can be disheartening for Leo. They thrive when they have a network of individuals who cheer them on and believe in their potential.

6. Insensitivity: Leos are sensitive individuals who value emotional connections. Being insensitive, dismissive, or neglecting the emotional needs of a Leo can be a major turn-off. It's important for partners to be attentive to their emotional cues and responsive to their feelings. Insensitivity can create a rift in a relationship and make Leo feel unappreciated.

7. Routine and Monotony: Leos enjoy excitement and variety in their lives. A turn-off for them is falling into a monotonous routine or feeling like their lives lack adventure and novelty. Repetitive and predictable activities can lead to boredom and restlessness in Leo. They are attracted to partners who can infuse their lives with new experiences and keep the spark alive.

8. Being Ignored: Leo's love being in the spotlight and receiving attention. Being ignored or overlooked in social settings or within a relationship can be a major turn-off. Leo individuals want to feel valued and heard, and they appreciate when their presence is acknowledged. Feeling invisible or unimportant can lead to feelings of frustration and unhappiness.

9. Lack of Romance: Leo individuals are often romantic at heart. A turn-off for them is a lack of romance or spontaneity in a relationship. They enjoy thoughtful gestures, surprise dates, and expressions of love. When a partner becomes complacent or neglects romantic aspects of the relationship, it can be disappointing for Leo. Keeping the romance alive and expressing love and affection is essential to keep Leo engaged.

10. Betrayal and Disloyalty: Loyalty is a core value for Leo individuals. A significant turn-off is experiencing betrayal or disloyalty from those they trust. Whether it's in friendships or relationships, Leo expects unwavering loyalty and trustworthiness. When their trust is broken, it can be emotionally devastating for Leo, leading to a breakdown in the relationship.

Understanding these turn-offs and taking steps to avoid them can contribute to healthier and more harmonious relationships with Leo individuals. Open communication and mutual respect are key to maintaining positive connections with Leo and ensuring they feel valued and appreciated.

let's delve into some specific turn-ons that are often associated with Leo individuals,

1. Admiration and Recognition:

Admiration and recognition are among the top turn-ons for Leo individuals. Leos thrive on being admired and appreciated for their unique qualities, talents, and achievements. When their partners and peers express genuine admiration and acknowledge their accomplishments, it sparks a profound attraction in Leo. Compliments, praise, and recognition are like fuel to their fiery personalities, and they feel deeply connected to those who celebrate their individuality.

2. Attention and Appreciation:

Leos are known for their vibrant personalities and their desire to be at the center of attention. They find it incredibly appealing when their partners give them undivided attention, especially in social settings. Being appreciated for their charisma and confident presence is a significant turn-on for Leo. Whether it's at a party or during an intimate conversation, showing genuine interest in what Leo has to say or do makes them feel cherished and drawn to their admirer.

3. Passionate Encounters:

Leos are intensely passionate individuals who approach life with enthusiasm and fervor. A significant turn-on for them is passionate and intense encounters, whether in love, romance, or physical intimacy. Leo individuals thrive on the intense emotions and energy that come from a deep connection with their partners. They find it highly attractive when their partners share their zeal and embrace life with the same level of passion. 4. Loyalty and Devotion:

Loyalty is a core value for Leo individuals, and they highly value the loyalty and devotion of their partners. Being in a relationship where their partner is unwaveringly loyal and dedicated to them is a powerful turn-on. Leo is attracted to those who stand by their side through thick and thin, providing emotional support and a sense of security. The depth of commitment and devotion in a relationship ignites Leo's passion and affection.

5. Confidence and Self-Assuredness:

Confidence is a trait that Leo individuals deeply appreciate in their partners. They find self-assured individuals highly attractive. Leo's own self-confidence is a defining characteristic, and they are drawn to those who exhibit a similar level of confidence. Partners who are secure in themselves, assertive, and unafraid to take the lead are particularly appealing to Leo.

6. Thoughtful Gestures:

Leo individuals are known for their romantic nature, and thoughtful gestures are a significant turn-on for them. Surprise dates, small gifts, love letters, and other considerate acts of affection ignite Leo's passion and love. They appreciate partners who take the time to plan special

101

moments and show their affection in creative and meaningful ways.

7. Shared Interests and Hobbies:

Leos highly value partners who share their interests and hobbies. Being with someone who enjoys engaging in creative or exciting activities together is a major turn-on for Leo. Shared adventures, whether it's dancing, traveling, or exploring new experiences, create a strong bond and ignite Leo's enthusiasm.

8. Spontaneity and Playfulness:

Leos are drawn to partners who bring spontaneity and playfulness into the relationship. They enjoy lighthearted moments, surprises, and a sense of adventure. Partners who keep the relationship exciting and fun are especially attractive to Leo.

9. Encouragement and Support:

Leo individuals appreciate partners who provide encouragement and support for their ambitions and creative pursuits. Being in a relationship where their dreams and goals are not only endorsed but actively encouraged is a significant turn-on for Leo. Partners who believe in their potential and support their endeavors are deeply cherished.

10. Emotional Connection:

Leo values emotional connections in their relationships. An intense emotional connection, where partners are attentive to their needs and responsive to their feelings, is a powerful turnon. Leo thrives in relationships where they feel deeply understood and emotionally connected to their partner.

These turn-ons provide insights into what attracts Leo individuals and sparks their passion and affection. While these preferences may vary from person to person, understanding and embracing these aspects can help create a stronger and more fulfilling connection with Leo partners. Open communication and a willingness to celebrate their unique qualities are key to fostering a deep and lasting attraction with Leo.

Preferred gifts

THAT ARE OFTEN APPRECIATED by Leo individuals

1. Personalized and Thoughtful Presents: Leos greatly appreciate personalized gifts that show thought and consideration. Something as simple as a customized piece of jewelry, a monogrammed accessory, or an item that reflects their unique interests or hobbies can make a significant impression. Personalized gifts demonstrate the effort put into choosing something special just for them, and Leo will cherish these tokens of affection.

2. Luxury and High-Quality Items: Leo individuals have a taste for luxury and often appreciate high-quality gifts. Consider gifting them items such as designer accessories, fine jewelry, or premium skincare products. These gifts align with Leo's love for the finer things in life and their desire to stand out with exceptional and elegant possessions.

3. Artistic and Creative Presents: Leos are known for their creative spirit and often enjoy artistic and creative gifts. You can consider gifting them artwork, a handmade craft, or a musical instrument if they have a penchant for music. These gifts tap into Leo's passion for self-expression and artistry, showing that you recognize and support their creative side.

4. Tickets to Events or Shows: Leos often enjoy being in the spotlight and experiencing exciting events. Gifting

them tickets to concerts, theater productions, sports games, or other live performances is a great choice. This allows them to indulge in their love for entertainment and can be a memorable and thrilling experience.

5. Stylish Fashion and Accessories: Leos take pride in their appearance and often have a keen sense of style. Gifting them fashionable clothing, accessories, or footwear can be a hit. Look for items that align with their tastes and make them feel confident and stylish.

6. Romantic Surprises: Leo individuals are romantic at heart and appreciate romantic gestures. Consider planning a surprise date, a romantic getaway, or a heartfelt love letter. These gestures tap into Leo's love for romance and passion, and they will treasure the effort you put into creating memorable moments.

7. Home Décor and Statement Pieces: Leo enjoys showcasing their unique style, even at home. Gifts like decorative statement pieces, artistic home décor, or elegant furniture can be appreciated. These items allow Leo to express their individuality and create a vibrant and stylish living space.

8. Spa and Wellness Treatments: Treat Leo to a day of relaxation and pampering with spa treatments, massages, or wellness packages. Leo's individuals appreciate self-care and rejuvenation, and these gifts allow them to unwind and feel their best.

9. Adventure and Travel Experiences: Leos often have a thirst for adventure and exploration. Consider gifting them a travel experience, whether it's a weekend getaway to a beautiful destination, an exciting adventure tour, or a hot

air balloon ride. These gifts align with Leo's love for excitement and new experiences.

10.Tech Gadgets and Entertainment: For tech-savvy Leo individuals, consider gifts like the latest gadgets, gaming consoles, or high-quality headphones. These items cater to their love for entertainment and can provide hours of enjoyment.

While these preferred gifts are likely to resonate with Leo individuals, it's important to keep in mind that each person is unique, and their specific tastes may vary. The key to selecting the perfect gift for a Leo is understanding their individual interests and desires. Thoughtfulness and personalization go a long way in making Leo feel appreciated and cherished.

Let's explore potential Adversaries to Leo individuals

1. Authoritarian Figures: Leo individuals value their independence and often find themselves at odds with authoritarian figures. They resist being controlled or dictated to and can be quite rebellious in the face of excessive authority. This adversarial dynamic often plays out in situations where Leo feels their freedom is compromised, whether in personal relationships or within hierarchical organizations.

2. Envious or Competitive Peers: Leos thrive on recognition and admiration. They can find themselves at odds with envious or highly competitive peers who may attempt to undermine their success or outshine them. This rivalry can lead to clashes in social or professional settings as Leo individuals don't take kindly to threats to their position in the spotlight.

3. Naysayers and Critics: Leos are known for their self-confidence and optimism. They often clash with individuals who consistently criticize, doubt, or express negativity about their ideas and goals. Leo's enthusiasm can wane when they have to deal with those who don't believe in their abilities or dismiss their aspirations.

4. Overly Controlling Partners: Leos value their independence and self-expression, making them susceptible to conflicts with overly controlling or possessive partners. A relationship where one partner tries to dominate or restrict Leo's actions and choices can lead to frustration and

clashes. Leo's desire for freedom may clash with their partner's need for control.

5. Conceited Individuals: Leo individuals have their fair share of self-confidence and can be put off by individuals who display excessive conceit or arrogance. Clashes may arise when they encounter someone who appears overly self-centered or dismissive of others' viewpoints. Leo appreciates confidence but not at the expense of humility.

6. Pessimists and Cynics: Leos are optimists by nature, and they may find it challenging to get along with individuals who consistently express pessimism and cynicism. The clash between their positive outlook and someone else's negative perspective can lead to frustration and differences in communication and values.

7. Those Who Underestimate Their Abilities: Leo individuals take pride in their capabilities and achievements. They can become adversarial with individuals who underestimate their talents or potential. Leo's determination and self-belief may lead them to prove their worth and capabilities to those who doubt them.

8. Inflexible Thinkers: Leos are open to creative solutions and innovation. They may find it challenging to connect with individuals who are rigid and inflexible in their thinking. Clashes can occur when Leo's adaptable and open-minded nature clashes with someone who refuses to consider alternative perspectives.

9. Those Who Disregard Their Creative Expression: Leo's creativity is a vital aspect of their identity. Adversarial relationships may develop when they encounter individuals

who dismiss or overlook their creative expressions. Leo values being recognized for their artistic and imaginative endeavors, and when these are not acknowledged, tension can arise.

10.Individuals Who Steal the Limelight: Leos often gravitate towards the spotlight and find it adversarial when they encounter individuals who consistently overshadow them or seek attention at their expense. Clashes may occur when Leo feels their own presence and achievements are diminished by someone who constantly seeks the center of attention.

While these adversarial dynamics may arise in Leo's interactions with others, it's essential to remember that individual differences and circumstances play a significant role in these conflicts. Open communication and finding common ground are key to resolving conflicts and maintaining positive relationships with Leo individuals.

Let's explore who tends to get along best with Leo individuals

1. Aries (March 21 - April 19): Leo and Aries share a strong and dynamic connection due to their fire element. They both have a natural enthusiasm for life, making their interactions vibrant and exciting. Aries appreciates Leo's leadership qualities, while Leo admires Aries' adventurous spirit. They enjoy taking on challenges together and can be a power couple when they join forces.

2. Sagittarius (November 22 - December 21): Leo and Sagittarius, both fire signs, have a magnetic attraction. They share a love for adventure, exploration, and a positive outlook on life. Sagittarius' free-spirited nature

complements Leo's desire for independence. They have fun-filled, lively relationships and can embark on exciting journeys together, both literally and metaphorically.

3. Gemini (May 21 - June 20): Leo and Gemini share a strong mental connection. Gemini's quick wit and adaptability resonate well with Leo's charm and charisma. Their conversations are engaging and lively, and they can enjoy each other's company for hours. Leo's confidence can boost Gemini's self-esteem, creating a harmonious partnership.

4. Libra (September 23 - October 22): Leo and Libra are both ruled by Venus, the planet of love and beauty. They appreciate the finer things in life and share a love for aesthetics and harmonious surroundings. Libra's diplomatic nature complements Leo's leadership skills, creating a balanced and attractive partnership. They often enjoy social gatherings and have a deep emotional connection.

5. Aquarius (January 20 - February 18): Leo and Aquarius have a dynamic and electric connection. They are both known for their independent spirits, and this shared trait allows them to give each other space when needed. Aquarius appreciates Leo's warmth and creativity, while Leo admires Aquarius' unique and innovative ideas. They often engage in intellectual conversations and enjoy stimulating one another.

6. Aries and Leo: A Dynamic Duo: Leo and Aries are both fire signs, and they share a natural synergy. They are enthusiastic, spontaneous, and full of energy. Aries admires Leo's self-confidence and leadership qualities, while Leo appreciates Aries' adventurous spirit. Together, they create a dynamic and action-oriented partnership. Both signs love

taking on challenges and embarking on exciting adventures, making them a power couple that thrives on excitement and achievement.

7. Sagittarius and Leo: Adventure Seekers: Leo and Sagittarius, another fiery pair, have a magnetic attraction to each other. Both signs are known for their love of adventure, exploration, and a positive outlook on life. Sagittarius' free-spirited and open-minded nature complements Leo's desire for independence and self-expression. They enjoy taking risks, embarking on exciting journeys, and living life to the fullest. Together, they create a lively and fun-filled partnership.

8. Gemini and Leo: Engaging Conversationalists: Leo and

Gemini have a strong mental connection. Gemini's quick wit, adaptability, and love for communication resonate well with Leo's charm and charisma. Their conversations are engaging, lively, and intellectually stimulating. Leo's confidence can boost Gemini's self-esteem, and they often find themselves enjoying each other's company for hours, whether discussing profound topics or engaging in playful banter.

9. Libra and Leo: Aesthetic Harmony: Leo and Libra share a special connection as they are both ruled by Venus, the planet of love and beauty. They appreciate the finer things in life and have a shared love for aesthetics and harmonious surroundings. Libra's diplomatic and compromising nature complements Leo's strong leadership skills. Together, they create a balanced and attractive partnership that often enjoys social gatherings, artistic pursuits, and deep emotional connections.

10.Aquarius and Leo: Dynamic Independence: Leo and Aquarius share a dynamic and electric connection. Both signs are known for their independent spirits, and this shared trait allows them to give each other space when needed. Aquarius appreciates Leo's warmth, creativity, and self-expression, while Leo admires Aquarius' unique and innovative ideas. They often engage in intellectual conversations, stimulating each other's minds and forming a partnership that values both individuality and intellectual connection.

While these zodiac signs tend to get along best with Leo individuals, it's essential to remember that individual compatibility can vary based on unique personalities and circumstances. Ultimately, the success of any relationship, whether with a fellow fire sign or another zodiac, depends on open communication, mutual respect, and a willingness to appreciate each other's differences.

Let's explore some of the attractive traits of Leo individuals

1. Confidence: One of the most attractive traits of Leo individuals is their unwavering self-confidence. They carry themselves with regal assurance, exuding an air of self-assuredness that draws people toward them. Leo's confidence is magnetic, making them appear poised and capable in various situations. This self-assured demeanor often captivates and impresses those around them.

2. Charisma: Leo individuals possess a natural charisma that makes them stand out in any crowd. Their magnetic charm and vibrant personalities light up a room and leave a lasting impression. People are often drawn to Leo's charisma, finding it difficult to resist their captivating presence. Leo's ability to engage and influence others is one of their most attractive qualities.

3. Generosity: Leos are known for their generosity and big hearts. They are often the first to help a friend in need or support a charitable cause. Their willingness to give to others and make those around them feel special is an endearing trait. Leo's generosity is a significant part of their attractiveness, as it reflects their caring and compassionate nature.

4. Leadership Qualities: Leo is a natural leader who takes charge with confidence and authority. Their strong leadership qualities are attractive to those who appreciate someone with a clear sense of direction and the ability to inspire others. Leo's ability to lead, guide, and take responsibility in various situations makes them stand out as leaders and motivators.

5. Creativity: Creativity flows through Leo individuals, and they often have a strong artistic streak. They enjoy expressing themselves through various forms of art, be it music, painting, or performing arts. Their creativity is captivating and often inspires those around them. Leo's artistic abilities and their desire to share their creative endeavors are highly attractive traits.

6. Passion: Leo individuals are intensely passionate. They approach life with enthusiasm and zeal, making them stand out in whatever they pursue. Their passion is infectious and can ignite the passions of those they interact with. This fervor for life and its many facets is an appealing quality that attracts people to Leo.

7. Determination: Once a Leo sets their mind on a goal, they pursue it with unwavering determination. Their persistence and dedication are admirable traits that draw others to them. Leo's ability to stay focused on their objectives and work tirelessly to achieve them is an attractive quality that demonstrates their commitment to success.

8. Loyalty: Loyalty is of utmost importance to Leo individuals. They are fiercely loyal to their friends and loved ones, often going to great lengths to support and protect them. Their unwavering loyalty is a trait that fosters deep and meaningful connections, making them highly attractive as dependable and devoted friends or partners.

9. Optimism: Leos have a sunny disposition and tend to see the glass as half full. Their positive outlook on life is infectious and can uplift the spirits of those around them. Leo's optimism is an attractive quality, as it brings an air of positivity and hope to any situation. It is reassuring to be in

the company of someone who exudes optimism even in challenging circumstances.

10.Courage: The lion is known for its courage, and this trait is mirrored in Leo individuals. They face challenges head-on and are not easily deterred by obstacles. Their bravery is an attractive quality that instills confidence and trust in their ability to handle adversity and stand up for what they believe in.

These attractive traits collectively make Leo individuals captivating and influential figures in the lives of those who have the privilege of knowing them. Whether in friendships, relationships, or leadership roles, Leo's combination of confidence, charisma, generosity, and creativity is a winning formula that makes them stand out and create lasting connections with others.

Negative traits

that may be associated with Leo individuals

1. Arrogance: One of the negative traits often associated with Leo individuals is arrogance. Their self-confidence can sometimes border on overconfidence, leading them to appear arrogant or conceited. Leo's belief in their abilities and their desire for recognition may lead them to downplay the contributions of others, which can be off-putting to those around them.

2. Stubbornness: Leo individuals are known for their determination, which can sometimes manifest as stubbornness. Once they set their sights on a goal or an idea, it can be challenging to persuade them to consider alternative viewpoints. Their unwavering commitment to their beliefs and decisions may lead to clashes with others who have different perspectives.

3. Self-Centeredness: Leo's natural inclination to seek attention and admiration can sometimes result in self-centered behavior. They may focus on their needs, desires, and achievements to the detriment of considering the feelings and viewpoints of others. This self-centeredness can strain relationships and lead to misunderstandings.

4. Impatience: Leo individuals are often driven by their desire for immediate results and success. Their impatience can lead to frustration when things don't progress as quickly as they'd like. This impatience may affect their ability to work collaboratively and can result in tension with those who have a more measured approach.

5. Pride and Ego: Leo's pride and ego can be both a strength and a weakness. While a healthy sense of pride can motivate them to excel, an overinflated ego can lead to difficulties in relationships. They may struggle with admitting mistakes or accepting constructive criticism, which can hinder personal and professional growth.

6. Demanding Attention: Leo's desire to be the center of attention can sometimes manifest as a need for constant validation. They may demand attention and recognition from others, which can be exhausting for those around them. This constant need for admiration can lead to conflicts in relationships.

7. Competitive Nature: While competitiveness can be a positive trait, Leo's competitive spirit can sometimes become a negative aspect. They may be overly competitive, even in situations where it's unnecessary or inappropriate. This competitive nature can strain relationships and create an environment of rivalry.

8. Prone to Drama: Leo individuals have a flair for the dramatic, which can lead to a tendency to exaggerate situations or react emotionally to minor issues. This penchant for drama can sometimes create unnecessary conflicts or amplify misunderstandings.

9. Intolerance for Criticism: Leo's strong sense of self and confidence can make them intolerant of criticism. They may react defensively or become upset when they receive feedback, even if it's intended to be constructive. This reluctance to accept criticism can hinder personal growth and effective communication.

10.Difficulty in Sharing the Spotlight: Leo's love for attention and recognition can lead to a reluctance to share the spotlight with others. In group settings or collaborations, they may dominate the conversation or take credit for collective achievements. This behavior can be a source of tension and conflict within teams.

It's important to note that these negative traits are not universal and may vary from one individual to another. Additionally, self-awareness and personal growth can help Leo individuals mitigate these negative aspects, allowing them to harness their positive qualities and build harmonious relationships with others.

Let's explore some of the things that Leo's individuals are often into

———

1. Creative Arts: Leo individuals have a strong affinity for creative arts. They are often into activities such as painting, drawing, music, and theater. Expressing themselves through artistic endeavors allows them to showcase their unique talents and bring their inner creativity to life. Many Leos find immense joy in producing and appreciating art in its various forms.

2. Entertainment and Performances: Leos have a natural love for entertainment and performances. They enjoy attending concerts, live theater productions, dance performances, and other live events. The thrill of being part of an audience and witnessing the talents of performers on stage is something that captivates Leo's heart. Their enthusiasm for entertainment often extends to participating in performances themselves, such as singing, acting, or dancing.

3. Fashion and Style: Leo individuals have a keen sense of style, and they are often into fashion. They appreciate wellcrafted clothing, accessories, and elegant ensembles that allow them to express their unique personality. Shopping, attending fashion shows, and curating their wardrobe are all activities that Leo may thoroughly enjoy.

4. Social Gatherings and Parties: Leos are naturally social beings, and they are into social gatherings and parties. They

love the excitement of mingling with friends and meeting new people. Hosting or attending parties and events, whether it's a grand celebration or an intimate get-together, is something that brings them great joy. Leo's charismatic nature often shines in social settings.

5. Leadership and Taking Charge: Leo individuals are into leadership roles and taking charge of situations. They are drawn to positions of authority, whether in their careers or personal lives. Leading and guiding others gives them a sense of purpose and fulfillment. Leo's natural leadership qualities often lead them to excel in roles that require direction and decision-making.

6. Fitness and Physical Activities: Staying active and taking care of their physical health is something that many Leo individuals are into. They often enjoy sports, fitness classes, and outdoor activities. Exercise not only helps them stay in shape but also provides an outlet for their boundless energy and enthusiasm.

7. Adventure and Travel: Leos have an adventurous spirit and are often into travel and exploring new destinations. They crave experiences that take them out of their comfort zone and into the world. Whether it's embarking on a spontaneous road trip or planning a grand international adventure, Leo individuals find fulfillment in the excitement of discovery.

8. Self-Expression and Individuality: Leo individuals are deeply into self-expression and celebrating their individuality. They often seek ways to stand out from the crowd and be recognized for their unique qualities. This may manifest through their clothing choices, hairstyle, or even through their hobbies and creative pursuits.

9. Luxury and Fine Dining: Leo individuals appreciate the finer things in life, and they are often into luxury experiences. They enjoy dining in upscale restaurants, savoring gourmet cuisine, and indulging in high-quality products and services. The opulence and extravagance associated with luxury appeal to their sense of grandeur.

10. Romance and Passion: Leo individuals are into romance and passion. They have a strong desire for love and affection and often engage in romantic pursuits. Candlelit dinners, heartfelt gestures, and memorable date nights are some of the things they cherish. Leo's amorous nature thrives on the excitement of love and the intense connection it brings.

These are just a few of the things that Leo individuals are often into. Keep in mind that individual preferences may vary, and not all Leos will share the same interests. However, the common thread that unites them is their enthusiasm, passion, and desire to lead fulfilling and vibrant lives.

Let's explore the compatibility of Leo with other zodiac signs,

1. Aries (March 21 - April 19): Leo and Aries share a strong and dynamic connection due to their fire element. Both signs have an innate enthusiasm for life and adventure,

121

and this shared energy ignites their compatibility. They often find themselves in sync, motivating and inspiring each other. Leo appreciates Aries' fiery spirit and leadership qualities, while Aries is drawn to Leo's confidence and charisma. Their passionate and adventurous natures create a harmonious and passionate union.

2. Taurus (April 20 - May 20): Leo and Taurus have a complex yet potentially rewarding compatibility. Taurus is practical and grounded, while Leo is fiery and energetic. They may initially clash due to their differing priorities, but over time, they can learn to complement each other. Taurus admires Leo's vitality, while Leo appreciates Taurus' stability. Their shared desire for luxury and comfort can create a strong bond if they find common ground.

3. Gemini (May 21 - June 20): Leo and Gemini have a lively and engaging compatibility. Both signs are social, communicative, and highly adaptable. They enjoy intellectual stimulation and can engage in fascinating conversations. Leo appreciates Gemini's quick wit and charm, while Gemini is drawn to Leo's confidence and charisma. They can have a fun and dynamic relationship as long as they balance their social pursuits with quality time together.

4. Cancer (June 21 - July 22): Leo and Cancer have differing approaches to life, which can make their compatibility challenging. Leo is outgoing, while Cancer is more nurturing and sensitive. However, when they understand and respect each other's differences, they can find common ground. Leo admires Cancer's caring nature, while Cancer appreciates Leo's warmth and protection. Building a

strong emotional connection and open communication is crucial for their compatibility.

5. Virgo (August 23 - September 22): Leo and Virgo have a compatibility that requires patience and understanding. Virgo is practical and detail-oriented, while Leo is expressive and enthusiastic. Their differing personalities can lead to clashes, but they can balance each other's strengths. Virgo admires Leo's confidence, while Leo values Virgo's organization and support. With effort, they can create a harmonious partnership by appreciating each other's qualities.

6. Libra (September 23 - October 22): Leo and Libra share a compatibility filled with love and romance. Both signs are ruled by Venus, the planet of love and beauty, which enhances their connection. They enjoy the finer things in life and appreciate aesthetics. Leo admires Libra's diplomacy and charm, while Libra is drawn to Leo's confidence and leadership. Their shared values and love for socializing create a delightful and harmonious relationship.

7. Scorpio (October 23 - November 21): Leo and Scorpio have a compatibility that's intense and passionate. Both signs are strong-willed and have a desire for power and control, which can lead to power struggles. However, if they learn to trust and respect each other, their connection can be deeply transformative. Leo admires Scorpio's intensity, while Scorpio values Leo's loyalty and protection. Their passionate connection can be both challenging and rewarding.

8. Sagittarius (November 22 - December 21): Leo and Sagittarius share a compatibility brimming with adventure and excitement. Both signs are fire signs, and their shared enthusiasm for life creates a dynamic and passionate

connection. They enjoy exploring new horizons, whether through travel or intellectual pursuits. Leo appreciates Sagittarius' free-spirited nature, while Sagittarius is drawn to Leo's confidence and charisma.

Their relationship is often filled with laughter and a zest for life.

9. Capricorn (December 22 - January 19): Leo and Capricorn have a compatibility that can be challenging but rewarding. Capricorn is practical and goal-oriented, while Leo is expressive and enthusiastic. They may have differing priorities, but they can find balance by respecting each other's strengths. Capricorn admires Leo's confidence, while Leo values Capricorn's stability and determination. Their relationship requires compromise and understanding to thrive.

10. Aquarius (January 20 - February 18): Leo and Aquarius have an electrifying and dynamic compatibility. Both signs are independent and value their freedom, which can create a harmonious partnership. They share a love for innovation and creative expression. Leo appreciates Aquarius' unique ideas, while Aquarius is drawn to Leo's warmth and leadership. Their relationship is marked by intellectual stimulation, shared adventures, and mutual support.

11. Pisces (February 19 - March 20): Leo and Pisces have a compatibility that blends Leo's strength with Pisces' sensitivity. They have the potential to create a deeply emotional and compassionate connection. Leo admires Pisces' creativity and intuition, while Pisces values Leo's confidence and protection. Their relationship can be marked by romantic gestures, empathy, and a shared dreaminess.

124

While these compatibility insights offer a general overview, it's essential to remember that individual relationships are unique, and many other factors, including personal experiences and life circumstances, can influence compatibility. Open communication, mutual respect, and a willingness to understand and embrace each other's differences play a significant role in making Leo's relationships successful with individuals of different zodiac signs.

Leos: The Fiery Drama Queens of the Zodiac

Leos, the fifth sign of the zodiac, are known for their fiery and exuberant personalities. Born between July 23 and August 22, they are the lovable drama queens of the zodiac. Their energy radiates with a distinct vibrancy and enthusiasm, making them impossible to overlook. In this cosmic exploration, we'll unveil the enigmatic personality traits that define the ferocious feline that is Leo. From their passionate nature to their innate need for the spotlight, we'll dive deep into what makes Leos the captivating individuals they are. So, if you have a Leo in your life, hold on tight as we journey through the traits, compatibility, characteristics, and much more that define this lion-hearted sign.

The Leo Zodiac Sign: The Fiery Lion

Leo, symbolized by the majestic lion, is a fire sign. This fiery nature is at the core of their being, fueling their passion, determination, and distinctive communication style. Leos are natural showmen, born to dazzle and sparkle as they embrace life on their own terms. While this magnetic energy often positions them in the spotlight, it's typically not driven by malice. Leo is deeply connected to their emotions, wearing their heart on their sleeve. Their quintessential trait is their heart's dominance over their head, leading to a rollercoaster of emotions. Bravery, vanity, romance, and drama are classic Leo characteristics. Yet, beneath the theatrics lies unwavering loyalty and a profound sense of protectiveness that runs deep.

The AstroTwins on Leo Energy

The AstroTwins describe Leo energy as "courageous, kind, generous, loyal, protective, nakedly honest, and entertaining." While their larger-than-life personalities might sometimes overshadow their quieter counterparts, the impact of Leo's energy can be transformative. It leaves others inspired and reinvigorated, encouraging them to break free from constraints and live life authentically.

Recognizing Leo's Presence

Astrologically conscious individuals can often identify a Leo shortly after meeting one. There's a distinct vibe that surrounds Leos, drawing others into their orbit like a magnetic force. They are the life of the party, the loudest karaoke singers, the most flamboyant dressers, and the boldest, most charismatic companions. Their unmistakable presence sets them apart in any crowd.

Leo's Best and Worst Traits

Leos are known for a range of personality traits, both positive and negative. When they are at their best, they are entertaining, flamboyant, passionate, expressive, bold, glamorous, warm, natural leaders, artistic, hilarious, faithful, fashionable, assertive, fearless, honest, and more. However, they can also exhibit negative traits, such as possessiveness, recklessness, callousness, show-offish behavior, domineering tendencies, being overbearing, spitefulness, jealousy, narcissism, sloppiness, self-centeredness, shallowness, infuriating attitudes, wrath, and vanity.

Leos as Friends

Leos make fantastic friends due to their loyalty, generosity, empowering nature, hospitality, caring disposition, friendliness, sunny outlook on life, party-loving spirit, creativity, and protective instincts. They radiate positivity and warmth, making them the life of any social gathering.

Leos as Lovers

In love, Leos are known for their sensuality, enthusiasm, flirtatious nature, hot-blooded passion, endless romantic gestures, bedroom prowess, generosity, stunning appearances, fiery personalities, dominating tendencies, exhibitionism, insatiable desires, wild imaginations, outrageous behaviors, friskiness, cockiness, swagger, and charm. They bring excitement and intensity to romantic relationships.

Leos in the Workplace

In professional settings, Leos are often seen as take-charge individuals, motivators, charismatic leaders, responsible workers, brave decision-makers, exceptional event planners, go-getters, capable managers, innovative thinkers, magnetic personalities, unwavering workers, efficient delegates, chatty colleagues, and more. They possess an inherent drive for success and leadership.

Leo's Style

Leo's style is characterized by boldness, flashiness, trend-setting fashion choices, exotic influences, luxurious preferences, and a confident demeanor. They have a unique sense of self-expression through their clothing and accessories.

Leo's Ideal Careers

Leos are well-suited for careers in acting, teaching, counseling, artistry, interior decoration, law, agency work, performance arts, religious leadership, CEO roles, event planning, human rights advocacy, children's literature, politics, public speaking, motivational training, dance, creative entrepreneurship, fashion design, game development, and animal training. Their innate leadership qualities and charisma are assets in various professional fields.

frequently asked questions about Leo, the vibrant and confident zodiac sign.

1. What are the key personality traits of a Leo?

Leos are known for their confidence, generosity, leadership qualities, charisma, and creative nature. They are passionate, determined, and optimistic individuals with a strong sense of loyalty to their loved ones.

2. What is Leo's ruling planet, and how does it influence their personality?

Leo is ruled by the Sun. The Sun represents warmth, vitality, and leadership. This celestial influence is reflected in Leo's confident and charismatic demeanor. They often shine as natural leaders and are drawn to roles of authority.

3. Are Leos attention-seekers?

Yes, Leos have a strong desire to be recognized and admired. They enjoy being the center of attention and appreciate compliments and recognition for their accomplishments. This attention-seeking quality is linked to their charismatic and extroverted nature.

4. What are some common career paths for Leo individuals?

Leos excel in careers that allow them to express their creativity and take on leadership roles. They are often found in the arts, entertainment, and creative industries. Many Leos thrive as actors, musicians, politicians, entrepreneurs, and public speakers.

5. What challenges do Leos face in relationships?

While Leos are loving and loyal partners, their confidence can sometimes come across as ego, which may create friction in relationships. They may also seek admiration and recognition from their partners, and if not received, it can lead to insecurity.

6. Do Leos make good friends?

Absolutely! Leos are known for their loyalty and their willingness to provide unwavering support to their friends. They are the friends you can count on in times of need and are often the life of the party, making them enjoyable company.

7. How do Leos handle challenges and setbacks?

Leos are known for their determination and courage. They face challenges head-on and persist with unwavering dedication. Their optimism and confidence help them overcome obstacles and turn setbacks into opportunities for growth.

8. What zodiac signs are most compatible with Leo?

Leos tend to be compatible with other fire signs like Aries and Sagittarius, as they share a similar enthusiasm and energy. They also have good compatibility with air signs like Gemini and Libra, which balance their fiery nature.

9. How can Leo individuals maintain a healthy balance between confidence and humility?

Leos can maintain this balance by practicing self-awareness and being mindful of their interactions with others. Cultivating humility and actively listening to different perspectives can help them avoid appearing overly self-centered or arrogant.

10. What famous personalities are Leos?

There are numerous famous Leo individuals, including actors like Daniel Radcliffe and Jennifer Lawrence, musicians like Madonna and Mick Jagger, and political figures like Barack Obama and Fidel Castro. Leos often gravitate toward careers that put them in the spotlight.

Leo Compatibility

Leo and Aries

Compatibility Overview (83%):

Passionate Connection (90%): Leo and Aries share a passionate and fiery connection. They have similar sexual preferences and a strong, energetic dynamic. Their strong personalities and intense love keep the relationship vibrant. However, occasional ego clashes can affect their confidence and libido.

Trust Issues (60%): Both Leo and Aries may have trust issues. They value loyalty and often feel possessive, leading to occasional jealousy. While they value each other highly, the possessiveness can be challenging to manage. Their mutual passion and determination help build trust over time.

Energetic Communication (90%): Their conversations are initially filled with energy, admiration, and respect. They quickly rebound from fights, and their sexual life blossoms afterward. They share common interests and appreciate each other's qualities.

Emotional Compatibility (99%): Emotionally, Leo and Aries are highly compatible. They both have strong Sun energy, representing love, warmth, and passion. Their

132

emotional connection is a significant strength of their relationship.

Shared Values (95%): Both appreciate conciseness and clarity in communication. However, power struggles for dominance in the relationship can create tension, as they both desire to be the leader.

Differing Activities (65%): Their daily routines and energy levels may differ, with Aries seeking excitement and Leo enjoying more relaxed activities. Finding common ground in shared activities may require compromise.

In summary, the Leo and Aries relationship is passionate and filled with occasional conflicts. They fight for their love daily, finding joy in the process, as their shared Fire element attracts them to the excitement and intensity in their relationship.

Leo and Taurus

Compatibility Overview (29%):

Sexual Dynamics (50%): The sexual relationship between Leo and Taurus can be exhausting due to their shared tendency to be lazy. Their differences in approaching intimacy can lead to personal satisfaction battles, making it essential for both partners to prioritize each other's needs.

Trust and Truth (60%): As fixed signs, Leo and Taurus understand the importance of honesty in a relationship. They value trust but must be willing to develop their moral boundaries independently. Trust issues may arise if they maintain behavioral patterns from previous relationships.

Communication and Intellect (5%): Their intellectual differences can create conflicts, with Taurus being practical and Leo holding onto their ego. A lack of flexibility in communication can lead to ongoing disagreements.

Emotional Disconnect (20%): While both are passionate signs, Leo and Taurus often don't fall in love with each other. They may struggle to connect emotionally and might remain in their separate worlds.

Differing Values (1%): Leo values bravery, inner fire, and the shiny aspects of life, while Taurus values financial security and material beauty. Their value systems are significantly different, which can lead to misunderstandings.

Shared Activities (40%): They can find common ground in simple activities like going to fancy restaurants. Their shared activities may not be extensive, but they can enjoy less demanding and physical endeavors together.

In summary, Leo and Taurus may face challenges due to their contrasting natures, but with patience and balance, they can create a unique partnership that helps them grow and enjoy each other's company.

Leo and Gemini

Compatibility Overview (82%):

Sexual Chemistry (90%): Leo and Gemini enjoy a stimulating sexual relationship. While Gemini brings ideas and excitement, Leo offers creativity and love. Their sex life can be energized by their intellect and communication. They can experiment and embrace their intimacy without shame.

Trust and Mutual Understanding (45%): Both Gemini and Leo may struggle with trust due to their tendency to focus on their own needs. It's crucial for them to prioritize each other's needs and establish trust by sharing and listening from the beginning of the relationship.

Communication and Intellect (95%): Gemini and Leo are both rational and focus on their mental activity. They appreciate each other's intellectual strengths, and their direct communication style builds trust. However, Leo's desire to impose their will can be a challenge.

Emotional Connection (85%): Leo's warmth and charm resonate with Gemini, sparking wonderful emotions. Their conscious nature leads to verbal displays of emotions, fostering a love story filled with support, respect, and continuous discussions.

Shared Values (99%): Both Leo and Gemini highly value intelligence, clarity, and independence. Leo appreciates Gemini's inner child, which aligns perfectly with their values.

Shared Activities (80%): Gemini's desire for various activities complements Leo's willingness to engage in diverse experiences. They find a balance between Gemini's active lifestyle and Leo's occasional need for rest, respecting each other's needs.

In summary, Leo and Gemini have the potential for a fun and joy-filled relationship. They may need to make small adjustments in their behavior to address their different approaches to change, but their mutual respect can help them build a strong foundation for their relationship.

Leo and Cancer

Compatibility Overview (29%):

Sexual Chemistry (30%): Leo and Cancer's sexual relationship can be challenging due to their different emotional depths. Leo's passion might scare Cancer, while Cancer's tenderness may not align with Leo's needs. They may need to find middle ground by listening to each other's needs.

Trust and Mutual Understanding (50%): Cancer might find Leo's need for attention and admiration irritating, which could affect their trust. Both partners need to prioritize trust and open communication to avoid secret searches for more compatible partners.

Communication and Intellect (10%): Cancer and Leo have differing communication styles due to the Moon-Sun dynamic. They may struggle to see eye to eye, but if they have respect for each other's approaches, they can learn from their differences.

Emotional Connection (45%): Cancer values deep emotional connections and Leo's need to shine may not align with this. Their opposing needs in relationships can challenge their emotional bond.

Shared Values (1%): Cancer and Leo have vastly different values. Cancer values tenderness, family, and stability, while Leo values passion, energy, and being in the spotlight. Their priorities do not align.

Shared Activities (35%): Leo's desire for public attention and

Cancer's preference for intimate settings can lead to conflicts in shared activities. Leo wants to be seen, while Cancer enjoys more private and cozy moments.

In summary, Leo and Cancer's relationship can be challenging due to their differences in communication, values, and emotional needs. While they have strengths as individuals, their connection may require compromise and understanding to thrive.

Leo And Leo

- Leo & Leo Sexual & Intimacy Compatibility (50%): The combination of two Leos can be challenging in terms of intimacy, as their passionate natures can sometimes create boundaries between them. While their sex life may seem exciting, there can be a tendency to hold onto their confident facades for too long, preventing them from connecting on a deeper level. They need to work on removing these barriers to achieve true intimacy.

- Leo & Leo Trust (70%): Leos are known for their confidence and open nature, but when two Leos come together, there can be a struggle for supremacy. This might lead to inflated stories and a need to prove themselves to each other. To build trust, they should learn to be fully present for each other and not engage in constant self-promotion.

- Leo & Leo Communication And Intellect

(65%): Two Leos have the potential to shed light on each other's important issues when they connect on a personal level. However, conflicts may arise when their egos clash, leading to disagreements over who is right. Finding a middle ground is essential to avoid prolonged, irrelevant disputes.

- Leo & Leo Emotions (90%): Leo is a Fire sign with a passionate nature, and while they might sometimes appear unemotional, they understand each other's emotional depth

140

perfectly. The challenge lies in expressing their feelings without getting burnt by their fiery personalities. If they can strike a balance, their emotional connection can be intense and fulfilling.

- Leo & Leo Values (99%): Two Leos share strong values, such as bravery, clarity, and inner strength. They both appreciate the importance of leisure and play in their lives, and they can enjoy their time together to the fullest. Their values align closely, creating a strong foundation for their relationship.

- Leo & Leo Shared Activities (85%): When it comes to shared activities, two Leos can lead a life of enjoyment and leisure. They often prefer spending time together, engaging in various activities and having fun. The only challenge may be their fixed nature, which can lead to differing approaches to routines. However, they should stay open to each other's suggestions to merge their worlds effectively.

In summary, a relationship between two Leos can be passionate and exciting, with the potential for deep emotional connection. However, they need to address issues related to boundaries, trust, and ego clashes to ensure a harmonious and longlasting partnership. Their shared values and love for leisure can be the cornerstone of their relationship.

Leo AND Virgo :

• Leo & Virgo Sexual & Intimacy Compatibility (5%):
Leo and Virgo, both rational signs, may find it challenging to
connect on an intimate level. Virgo's cautious and shy nature
can clash with Leo's desire to feel special and confident. Leo's
passionate approach might make Virgo feel unprotected and
insecure. The rationality of both signs may lead to an
intellectual battle for sexual dominance, making it difficult to
achieve true intimacy.

• Leo & Virgo Trust (65%): Trust should not be a
major issue for two conscious individuals like Leo and Virgo.
However, Leo's tendency to show off and project themselves
as dominant can affect Virgo's trust, especially if their
communication doesn't compensate for the confidence lost.
Maintaining respectful communication is vital for building
and maintaining trust in this relationship.

• Leo & Virgo Communication And Intellect (50%):
Both Leo and Virgo are ruled by rational, conscious planets,
making them easy to communicate with. However, their
differing elements, with Leo being Fire and Virgo being
Earth, create differences in their communication styles. Leo is
passionate and fiery, while Virgo is practical and intellectual.
They need to be respectful and tolerant of each other's
approach to maintain a harmonious connection.

• Leo & Virgo Emotions (1%): Leo and Virgo struggle
to achieve emotional closeness. Their rational natures and
differing expressions of affection create a challenge in
connecting on a deep emotional level. Leo shows affection
through passionate warmth, while Virgo tends to be shy and

expresses love through care, which may not align with Leo's confident demeanor.

- Leo & Virgo Values (35%): Both Leo and Virgo value intelligence and the ability to use one's mind. Leo admires someone's mind, and Virgo can provide that if they are open enough to show it. Their shared professional interests can create an environment where they can collaborate effectively. However, differences in their values, with Leo valuing grandeur and Virgo valuing humility, may pose challenges.

- Leo & Virgo Shared Activities (55%): Leo and Virgo can engage in shared activities despite their apparent differences. Their roles in the zodiac support cooperation, and Virgo can be a great partner for Leo if ego-related issues are minimal. Mutual respect is essential for their success, whether it's behind closed doors or in a more public setting. Leo seeks attention from their surroundings, while Virgo prefers to work behind the scenes, attending to details that contribute to their shared success.

In summary, Leo and Virgo form a partnership with a strong emphasis on rationality and practicality. However, their emotional connection is often lacking, and their search for perfection may lead them to believe they don't belong together. While they can work together effectively in professional or shared activities, forming a strong emotional or sexual bond is rare in this relationship.

Leo AND Libra

• Leo & Libra Sexual & Intimacy Compatibility (90%):
Leo and Libra have a healthy sex life filled with mutual
respect and a desire to explore new things together. Leo's
confidence and Libra's sexuality inspire each other to become
great lovers. While they may maintain public decorum, any
restrictions only serve to heighten their passion, and they will
seek moments of intimacy whenever they can. The Sun's rule
over Leo and Libra's representation of the public eye
influence their sexual preferences and behavior.

• Leo & Libra Trust (40%): Building mutual trust can
be challenging for Leo and Libra. They have differing
understandings of the Sun, with Leo ruling it and Libra being
its fall. The need for approval and the desire to be seen in
distinct ways can lead to jealousy and mistrust. To maintain
trust, they need to find approval and an attentive audience in
each other and avoid seeking it from external sources.

• Leo & Libra Communication And Intellect (85%):
Leo and Libra's communication is usually harmonious due to
the supportive sextile between their Suns. Their rationality
and respect for each other's ideas help them build stronger
personalities. However, Libra's jealousy of Leo's confidence
can disrupt their communication if they start making
assumptions and judgments. Maintaining mutual respect is
crucial for the success of their intellectual partnership.

• Leo & Libra Emotions (99%): Leo and Libra are
deeply in love and have strong emotions for each other. Their
connection is evident, and their belief in love leads them
towards marriage and a future together. Ruled by the Sun and

Venus, they follow a love cycle connected to eight years, and if they stay together beyond that, they may commit to marriage and building a family.

- Leo & Libra Values (75%): Leo values strong personalities, pride, and heroism, while Libra values justice and being the hero. They complement each other well, helping each other express their abilities and strengths. However, their differing relationships with Saturn, with Leo representing its detriment and Libra exalting it, can create challenges. Leo needs to become more responsible to meet Libra's value of reliability and tact.

- Leo & Libra Shared Activities (60%): Leo and Libra have a similarity in their speed, which may appear slower than expected for their elements (Fire and Air). They enjoy "red carpet" events and fancy gatherings where they can display themselves to the world. However, Libra's indecisiveness can be a source of conflict if Leo loses patience and takes over decisions. Maintaining independence and giving each other time is essential for their shared activities.

In summary, Leo and Libra's relationship involves the beautiful and challenging dignities of Saturn and the Sun. They have much to learn from each other, aiming for shared respect and responsibility in a balanced power dynamic. Their desire for competition may arise, but their relationship can still be enjoyable and something to showcase in public.

Leo AND Scorpio

Leo & Scorpio Sexual & Intimacy Compatibility (5%): The Leo and Scorpio relationship is marked by their strong personalities and a high sex drive. Leo tends to be passionate and casual in their approach to sex, while Scorpio embodies deep, emotional sensuality. Finding middle ground between their sexual preferences is a significant challenge, and their lack of emotional connection hinders their intimacy.

- Leo & Scorpio Trust (65%): Leo and Scorpio share a fixed quality, which fosters mutual trust. Establishing a transparent foundation at the beginning of their relationship helps build trust. However, the success of their trust depends on both partners' willingness to be open and honest.

- Leo & Scorpio Communication And Intellect (30%): Leo and Scorpio can have civilized conversations, as both value respect and share a degree of obsession in their pursuits. If they have common passions, they can engage in deep discussions and provide each other with what they need emotionally.

- Leo & Scorpio Emotions (1%): Leo and Scorpio experience a challenging emotional connection. They may display love in its negative form, as their relationship can be torturous and filled with negative emotions. Despite unhappiness, they may be bound by their emotions and fear of being wrong.

- Leo & Scorpio Values (35%): Both partners value honesty and clarity, but they interpret these values differently.

146

Finding a bridge in unconditional honesty is essential, as they grapple with the value of creation versus destruction.

- Leo & Scorpio Shared Activities (40%): Leo and Scorpio might engage in shared activities despite differing interests. Leo's understanding of Mars, Scorpio's ruling planet, allows them to cooperate well and have fun together. However, discrepancies in their perspectives on circumstances and people can pose challenges.

In summary, Leo and Scorpio face a complex relationship. They must understand each other's emotional expressions and respect each other's diverse needs. While their differences may initially seem insurmountable, they both seek unity in their own ways, and recognizing this shared goal can help their relationship thrive.

Leo AND Sagittarius

Leo & Sagittarius Sexual & Intimacy Compatibility (99%): Leo and Sagittarius, both fire signs, share a passionate and liberating sexual connection. Their intimacy is marked by warmth, respect, and a sense of liberation. This strong sexual bond can create a perfect connection between them.

• Leo & Sagittarius Trust (80%): Leo and Sagittarius boost each other's sense of security and confidence, leading to a strong sense of trust. Their mutual trust is usually stable unless their emotional connection wanes.

• Leo & Sagittarius Communication And Intellect (85%): Both Leo and Sagittarius are highly focused on mental activity, making them excellent communicators. They share a strong passion for intellectual discussions and are open to each other's opinions and convictions. Their relationship is characterized by deep and inspiring conversations.

• Leo & Sagittarius Emotions (80%): As two fire signs, Leo and Sagittarius display their emotions openly and passionately. They love to show their affection and can be quite intense in their expressions. Their love is warm and cuddly, and they often need to find a balance between their fiery emotions.

• Leo & Sagittarius Values (65%): Leo and Sagittarius both value strength of character and passion. They admire each other's courage and individuality. However, they may differ in their approaches to certain values and priorities.

- Leo & Sagittarius Shared Activities (40%): While both signs have a desire for adventure and knowledge, they may not always share the same pace and destinations when it comes to travel and activities. Their interests and approaches to shared activities may vary, but they can make it work if they add purpose and flexibility to their plans.

In summary, Leo and Sagittarius form a passionate and inspiring connection with a strong level of trust. They enjoy intellectual conversations and value each other's strengths. However, they must find a balance in their emotional intensity and be open to adapting their shared activities to make their relationship thrive.

Leo AND Capricorn

Leo & Capricorn Sexual & Intimacy Compatibility (5%):
Leo and Capricorn have very different approaches to
intimacy and sexuality. Their attraction to each other is
unlikely, and their sexual compatibility is low due to their
contrasting preferences and priorities.

- Leo & Capricorn Trust (40%): Trust can be a delicate
issue in a Leo and Capricorn relationship. They tend to see
through each other's motives, and this can lead to suspicion
and mistrust. However, in certain situations, they might find
reasons to trust each other.

- Leo & Capricorn Communication And Intellect
(60%): Their communication can be challenging due to
conflicting priorities. Leo and Capricorn have strong
individual agendas and may spend time trying to persuade
each other about what should come first. Respecting each
other's differences is crucial for satisfying communication.

- Leo & Capricorn Emotions (1%): Emotionally, Leo
and Capricorn face significant challenges. Leo's warm
emotions can be dampened by Capricorn's need for
seriousness and practicality. In turn, Capricorn's slow
approach to building emotional connections may clash with
Leo's fiery nature. Finding the right balance can be difficult.

- Leo & Capricorn Values (50%): They share common
values related to organization, plans, and presentations.
However, Leo's preference for openhearted and enthusiastic
individuals can clash with Capricorn's more reserved

demeanor. Their values may differ, affecting their compatibility.

- Leo & Capricorn Shared Activities (5%):

Shared activities depend on their current priorities, which may not align. Leo and Capricorn may resist doing things the other person wants to do, leading to a lack of shared interests and activities.

In summary, Leo and Capricorn have significant differences in their approach to intimacy, emotions, and communication. Finding common ground and shared activities can be challenging due to their contrasting priorities. Trust and emotional compatibility may also be issues they need to address.

Leo AND Aquarius

Leo & Aquarius Sexual & Intimacy Compatibility (99%): The attraction between Leo and Aquarius is intense and passionate. Their sexual relationship is a unique blend of liberation, warmth, and sensuality. They share an incredible experience that is both liberating and exciting, creating a strong connection based on the gravitational pull between the Sun and Uranus.

• Leo & Aquarius Trust (75%): Trust can be a challenge in a Leo and Aquarius relationship. Despite their strong connection, they may struggle with trust and the search for truth within their partnership. Separation often reveals how little they truly knew about each other.

• Leo & Aquarius Communication And Intellect (90%): Both Leo and Aquarius have strong personalities and a heroic approach to life. Their communication can be satisfying, but they may engage in unnecessary ego battles over dominance. Finding common ground is essential to channel their energy effectively.

• Leo & Aquarius Emotions (99%): Leo's warmth and Aquarius's unique emotional approach complement each other. When Leo falls in love, their passion is palpable, and Aquarius finds a safe haven in their fiery arms. Ego battles are the only threat to their emotional connection.

• Leo & Aquarius Values (80%): Both Leo and Aquarius highly value individuality. They are attracted to strong characters who know what they want. This common

152

value strengthens their connection, even if they disagree on many other matters.

- Leo & Aquarius Shared Activities (90%): Leo and Aquarius both enjoy showing off in their unique ways. They need to establish territories for self-expression, allowing each other to shine. It's essential for Leo to let Aquarius lead when circumstances are in the latter's favor. This dynamic keeps the relationship dynamic and harmonious.

In summary, Leo and Aquarius have a powerful and creative connection. They are capable of achieving remarkable things together if they can let go of unnecessary ego battles and find a shared cause to support. While their differences are significant, the potential for a deep and loving relationship exists if they focus on the outer world while nurturing their inner emotional bond.

Leo AND Pisces:

- Leo & Pisces Sexual & Intimacy Compatibility (1%): Leo and Pisces, despite both representing love, often struggle in forming an intimate relationship. Leo may come across as selfish and uninterested in intimacy, leaving Pisces feeling neglected. Their sexual roles and characters are too different for a satisfying sexual relationship.

- Leo & Pisces Trust (1%): Trust is a significant challenge in a Leo and Pisces relationship. Their characters may seem unreal to each other, leading to mistrust and misunderstanding. They may struggle to believe in each other's sincerity.

- Leo & Pisces Communication And Intellect (35%): While Leo and Pisces share creative interests, Leo's approach may shatter Pisces' ideals. Leo's criticism can affect Pisces' confidence and perception of the world. To create a safe environment, they should focus on their individual interests.

- Leo & Pisces Emotions (15%): Both Leo and

Pisces are highly emotional, but their expressions of emotion differ. Leo is passionate and ready to fight for their loved ones, while Pisces is more passive. These differences can lead to conflicts and misunderstandings.

- Leo & Pisces Values (20%): Despite having individual sets of beliefs, Leo and Pisces value clarity and honesty. They find common ground in Leo's heroic nature and Pisces' idealizing tendencies.

- Leo & Pisces Shared Activities (10%): Leo's fixed nature and Pisces' mutability make it challenging for them to synchronize their need for changes and new activities. Their different preferences for routine and change can create tension in their shared activities.

In summary, Leo and Pisces face significant challenges in their relationship due to their differences. They may struggle with trust, communication, and emotional compatibility. Their connection is complicated by the fall of Neptune in Leo's sign. Building a harmonious relationship would require understanding and acceptance of each other's unique qualities and focusing on the positive aspects of their connection.

Conclusion:

As we draw the final curtain on our exploration of the Leo zodiac sign, we hope you've discovered the essence of the Lion's heart and soul. In these pages, we've unraveled the mysteries, celebrated the strengths, and embraced the uniqueness that defines Leos. Whether you're a passionate Leo yourself or an enthusiastic reader on a quest for zodiac knowledge, we trust that this book has provided you with valuable insights and inspiration.

Leos, you have delved deep into the core of your personality, and we hope this book has illuminated your path, helping you embrace your strengths and navigate your challenges. For our other readers, we trust you've gained a newfound appreciation for the dynamic and charismatic Leos in your life.

We end this book with the realization that the Leo zodiac sign embodies a magnetic blend of strength, warmth, and creativity. Leo's influence extends far beyond the boundaries of the zodiac, inspiring us all to embrace our passions, lead with love, and shine as brightly as the Sun itself.

Thank You to Our Valued Readers:

As we close the pages of this book dedicated to the Leo zodiac sign, we want to take a moment to express our deepest gratitude to you, our cherished readers. Your curiosity, enthusiasm, and willingness to explore the world of astrology have made this endeavor truly rewarding.

We understand that your time and attention are precious, and we are genuinely thankful that you chose to embark on this astrological journey with us. The zodiac, with all its mysteries and wonders, holds a unique fascination for those who seek to understand themselves and the people around them better. Your dedication to this pursuit is both admirable and inspiring.

This book is just one star in the vast constellation of the zodiac, and we have many more awaiting your exploration. From Aries to Pisces, we invite you to continue your astrological journey with us as we delve into the intricacies of each sign, offering insights and guidance for your path.

Contact the astrologer

If you wish to dive deeper into the cosmos of astrology, seeking personal consultations or further information, we're here to assist you. Feel free to reach out to us at:

Phone: +1 829-205-5456 WhatsApp Email: danielsanjurjo47@gmail.com

Your feedback, questions, and insights are always welcome, and we look forward to helping you discover the unique qualities of each zodiac sign.

As you continue your voyage through the cosmos of astrology, we wish you a future filled with clarity, self-discovery, and the ever-present wisdom of the stars. The Leo zodiac sign has shared its radiant light with us, and we hope you carry that luminosity with you on your journey.

Once again, thank you for being a part of this incredible voyage. We appreciate your readership, your curiosity, and your shared passion for the zodiac.

With heartfelt thanks,

Daniel   Sanjurjo

**Did you love *Leo 2024*? Then you should read
Astrology Unveiled: Your Guide to the Zodiac[1] by The
fun book creators!**

Unlock the Mysteries of the Cosmos with "Celestial Wisdom:

An Astrologer's Journey"

☐ Are you ready to embark on a profound astrological journey that will illuminate your path to self-discovery, personal growth, and decision-making? "Celestial Wisdom: An Astrologer's Journey" is your definitive guide to the enchanting world of astrology.

□ Explore the Foundations of Astrology: Delve into the origins of astrology, the celestial bodies that influence our lives,

and the intricate language of the zodiac. From the sun signs to birth charts, this book unravels the enigma of the stars.

□ Debunking Myths and Discovering Realities: Address common misconceptions and criticisms surrounding astrology while gaining a deeper understanding of the scientific perspective on this ancient practice. Let the stars guide you on your path to wisdom.

□ In-Depth Zodiac Sign Insights: Embark on a journey through the twelve zodiac signs, each filled with tailored insights, predictions, and guidance for every aspect of life. The zodiac's influence on your personality, career, love life, and more will be unveiled.

□ Resources for Further Study: If you're eager to explore astrology beyond the pages of this book, our comprehensive resource section offers a guide to books, websites, and courses that will enrich your astrological knowledge.

□ Conclusion and Beyond: Conclude this mesmerizing voyage through the cosmos with a heartfelt reflection on the enduring wisdom of astrology. Unearth the stories the stars have written for you.

□ We encourage you to continue your exploration of the celestial realms, seeking the wisdom of the cosmos to guide your unique path. Your journey has only just begun.

This illustrated guide invites you to embrace the wisdom of the stars and unlock the tapestry of your life. Are you ready to embrace "Celestial Wisdom"? The universe awaits your discovery.

Also by Daniel Sanjurjo

Zodiaco

Piscis 2024: Un Viaje Celestial

Zodiac world

Aries Revealed 2024

Taurus 2024 Leo 2024

Gemini 2024

Cancer Zodiac Sign 2024

Virgo 2024

Scorpio 2024

Sagittarius 2024 Horoscope

Capricorn Unveiled: A Cosmic Guide to 2024

Aquarius Horoscope 2024

Standalone

The Dreams Interpretation Book

About the Author

Daniel Sanjurjo is a passionate author who delves into the realms of astrology and self-help. With a gift for exploring the celestial and the human psyche, Daniel's books are celestial journeys of self-discovery and personal growth. Join the cosmic odyssey with this insightful writer.